The Poetry of Alfred de Musset

Studies in the Humanities
Literature — Politics — Society

Guy Mermier, General Editor

Vol. 6

PETER LANG
New York · Bern · Frankfurt am Main · Paris

Lloyd Bishop

The Poetry of Alfred de Musset

Styles and Genres

PETER LANG
New York · Bern · Frankfurt am Main · Paris

Library of Congress Cataloging-in-Publication Data

Bishop, Lloyd.
  The poetry of Alfred de Musset.

  (Studies in the humanities ; v. 6)
  Bibliography: p.
  Includes index.
  1. Musset, Alfred de, 1810–1857—Criticism and
interpretation. I. Title. II. Series: Studies in
the humanities (New York, N.Y.) ; v. 6.
PQ2372.B57 1987   841'.7   86-21069
ISBN 0-8204-0357-1
ISSN 0271-6712

CIP-Kurztitelaufnahme der Deutschen Bibliothek

Bishop, Lloyd:
The Poetry of Alfred de Musset : styles and genres /
Lloyd Bishop.—New York ; Bern ; Frankfurt am
Main : Lang, 1987.
  (Studies in the humanities ; Vol. 6)

ISBN 0-8204-0357-1
NE: GT

© Peter Lang Publishing, Inc., New York 1987

Printed by Weihert-Druck GmbH, Darmstadt (West Germany)

to Lloyd and Norris—
children who make me proud to be a father

CONTENTS

PREFACE

While the bibliography on Alfred de Musset is extensive, book-length studies on Musset's poetry, except for a number of unpublished doctoral dissertations, are rare. The surprising fact is that only two books up to now have focussed exclusively on Musset's poetry: Jean d'Aquitaine's *Alfred de Musset: l'oeuvre, le poète*, published some eighty years ago, and Valentine Brunet's *Le Lyrisme d'Alfred de Musset dans ses poésies*. The latter, written over fifty years ago, is an earnest but rather sterile exercise in old-fashioned source criticism ("Had Musset read Shelley before writing poem X?"). Philippe Soupault's book on Musset, although appearing in the *Poètes d'aujourd'hui* series, is not a study of the poetry *per se* but of the poet's personality and is simply an "invitation" or call-for a serious re-examination of the poet. Most of the books dealing with Musset have been written in the *vie et oeuvre* format, in which the study of the poetry is necessarily brief since the critic must also treat the fictional and dramatic work as well as the biography. The result has been that Musset's poetry is blurred by infrequently examined assumptions. The conventional wisdom sees Musset solely as the writer of intensely personal lyric poetry. Musset's poetry? One thinks of the four *Nuits*, of *Souvenir* and *Rolla*, perhaps of *A la Malibran*, *L'Espoir en Dieu* and the *Lettre à M. de Lamartine*, and a few shorter pieces, the sonnet "Tristesse" for example. My hope is that this book on Musset's poetry, the first such study published by an American scholar, will reveal to the public a poet who wrote in many different genres and in many different styles.

Part One consists of four chapters and offers an overview of Musset's poetry and his poetics. Chapter one deals with Musset's first manner—the flamboyant romanticism of the *Contes d'Espagne et d'Italie*, and analyzes themes, characterization, versification, diction, imagery and various stylistic strategies of the long narrative and dramatic poems and the shorter pieces (e.g., the *chanson*, the sonnet, the ballad). Also studied is the volume's originality within the romantic movement as a whole.

Chapter two offers a survey of Musset's poetry after 1830 and focuses on the various genres: the shorter pieces (sonnet, rondeau, madrigal, *chanson*, romance, ballad, epigram, epistle, *billet*, *impromptu*) and especially the narrative, dramatic, lyric and satirical poetry. The chapter concludes with some "generalities" on Musset's poetic style, or rather, styles. Several times during the course of the chapter I have occasion to demonstrate the little known fact that there is in Musset's opus a substantial poetry of ideas.

Chapter three offers a new look at Musset's poetics and shows that there is more to it than an *esthétique du sentiment*. Ideas play an important role in Musset's conception of the goal of poetry and of the way good poets write.

Chapter four, "Musset's World: A Trembling Universe in Perpetual Motion," is an essay in thematic and phenomenological criticism. I attempt to reach the center of Musset's consciousness and of his imaginative universe through a careful study of recurring images, obsessive themes and fundamental stylistic tendencies.

Part Two offers four detailed stylistic studies. Chapter five presents an analysis of Musset's first sonnet. Chapter six studies romantic irony in *Namouna*. Chapter seven is a generic study of *Souvenir*; it situates the poem within the tradition of what Myer Abrams has called "the greater Romantic lyric." (Another poem that belongs to the genre—*Souvenir des Alpes*—is studied briefly from this generic perspective in an appendix.) Chapter eight focuses not on a single poem but on two significant tendencies of the entire opus: musicality and euphony. Dozens of critics have alluded to the musicality of Musset's verse but have generally confined their remarks to a one or two-sentence generalization. I approach the topic through close analysis of specific texts and then offer an objective method of handling the slippery subject of euphony.

Part Three consists of a single chapter. I review the various kinds of critical reaction to Musset's poetry, not to adjudicate between them, but to see by what codes and conventions Musset has been read and judged. I discuss not only cognitive codes in Jonathan Culler's sense but also aesthetic codes based on various critical approaches (emotional criticism, moralistic criticism, mimetic criticism, aesthetic criticism) and sexual reading codes (if the meaning of a literary text is the experience of a reader, what difference does it make if the reader of a poet like Musset is a woman?)

I have two hopes for this book. One is that it will reveal a poet whose work cannot be reduced to a sentimental *cri de coeur* and whose poetics cannot be reduced to an *esthétique du sentiment*. Another is that it will provide closely reasoned discussions of subjects rarely discussed in French letters: romantic irony, the greater Romantic lyric, musicality and euphony.

ACKNOWLEDGEMENTS

I gratefully acknowledge the help and encouragement of several friends and colleagues, especially Professor Robert Denommé of the University of Virginia and Professor James Hamilton of the University of Cincinnati. Special thanks are owed to Angie Harvey and Anita Malebranche for their technical assistance and expertise.

In another form, parts of this book have appeared in *The French Review*, *The Romanic Review* and *Nineteenth-Century French Studies*. I wish to thank the copyright holders for permission to reprint "Phonological Correlates of Euphony,"©1975 by the American Association of Teachers of French, in *The French Review*, 49 (1975), 11-22; "Romantic Irony in Musset's *Namouna*," © 1979 by T. H. Goetz in *Nineteenth-Century French Studies*, 7 (1979), 181-91; "Musset's First Sonnet: A Semiotic Analysis," © 1983 by the Trustees of Columbia University in *The Romanic Review*, 74 (1983), 455-460; "Musset's *Souvenir* and the Greater Romantic Lyric," © 1984 by T.H. Goetz in *Nineteenth-Century French Studies*, 12 (1984), 119-130. A portion of chapter eight will appear in *Language and Style*, 18 (1986) as "Euphony: A New Method of Analysis." I should also like to thank Presses Universitaires de France for its permission to reprint phonetic charts from the *Dictionnaire de Poétique et de Rhétorique* by Henri Morier. (Copyright © 1975 by Presses Universitaires de France).

PART ONE
Styles and Genres; Poetics and Poetic Vision

chapter one
MUSSET'S FIRST MANNER:
FLAMBOYANT ROMANTICISM

Published in 1830, several weeks before the première of Hugo's *Hernani*, the *Contes d'Espagne et d'Italie* are the culmination of a stylistic revolution in French poetry. Musset did not start the revolution, he joined a revolution in progress. But in joining it he contributed something of his own. The importance of Musset's contribution to the romantic movement is not diminished by the fact that he was soon to desert it. As Emmanuel Barat has stated: "*Les Contes d'Espagne et d'Italie* ont pour nous une importance unique: c'est la première oeuvre dont l'auteur n'ait pas débuté par des vers pseudo-classiques. Lamartine et Vigny devaient rester toute leur vie des hommes de style ancien" (*Style poétique*, p. 217).

Musset has a "style" in the *Contes* mainly because he has made a choice: he has chosen to follow the new romantic lead and reject the neo-classical training he had received in school. One cannot speak of him as having forged for himself a unique style in the sense of an idiolect; but, as Roman Jakobson and Roland Barthes have both suggested, poetic language, like all language, is socialized, it never engenders a totally distinct idiolect. An author's style is always pervaded by certain verbal patterns coming from the community of which he fancies himself a part, even if that community is a small band of revolutionaries. In the *Contes* Musset is writing to please his fellow romantics and in the process of course to startle the stodgy bourgeois and to enrage the greying classicist. But the romantic code was elastic and eclectic, it was founded on an aesthetics of freedom rather than constraint, and thus Musset was enabled to contribute his own stone to the edifice.

The basic style of the *Contes* can be called flamboyant romanticism, as Pierre Gastinel has labeled Musset's entire first period or manner. First, the choice of setting: the cool, classical atmosphere of ancient Greece and Rome are replaced by the hot passions and climate of Spain and modern Italy. While near France geographically, Italy and Spain have always been exotic to the French in both atmosphere and temperament, especially in the stereotypes that the romantics forged for themselves from secondary sources. At this point in his career Musset's knowledge of Italy as well as Spain was purely literary. It was Byron especially who oriented the young French poet toward Spain. In *Childe Harold* Byron had praised the eyes of the Spanish girl ("darker than the black tissue of her veil");

the frail, pale beauties of the North simply could not compare. Musset had also read *La Dolorida* (Vigny, 1823), *Le Théâtre de Clara Gazul* (Mérimée, 1825), Emile Deschamps's *Les Études françaises et étrangères* (1828) and of course Hugo's *Odes et ballades* and the *Orientales*. His interest in Spain was undoubtedly heightened by his interest in the Spanish *comedia* of the Golden Age. He had read Tirso de Molina's *El burlador de Sevilla y convidado de piedre* and Lope's *El perro del hortelano*. In his essay on tragedy he will express admiration for Calderón, from whom he borrowed the title of one of his most important plays (*No hay burlas con el amor*).[1]

Spain for Musset was a country of sensual luminosity and bright colors, picturesque architecture and picaresque mores. It was also the homeland of intense, excessive emotions: burning passions, ferocious jealousy and revenge, the point of honor that can turn a lover into a killer. The plot of *Don Paez* can serve as paradigm for all the tales of jealousy and revenge: Don Paez learns that his mistress, La Juana, is sharing her favors with another young soldier. The two men agree that only one of them should remain alive but also that the one who survives the dual of honor must kill the unfaithful mistress. Don Paez kills his rival and buys a slow-working poison that will give him just enough time to kill his mistress.

Italy for Musset is a country that rhymes with folly—

> . . . Italie,
> Voyez-vous, à mons sens, c'est la rime à folie.[2]
> (*Marrons du feu*)

> Et qui, dans l'Italie
> N'a son grain de folie?
>   ("Venise")

> Aimable Italie,
> Sagesse ou folie,
> Jamais ne t'oublie
> Qui t'a vue un jour.
>   ("La Cantate de Bettine")

Musset's Italy is a frivolous paradise of spontaneous, uninhibited joy, a country where according to Stendhal one should be concerned only with making music and love (*Rome, Naples et Florence*). Byron again, Shakespeare and the memoirs of Casanova contributed to Musset's love of a country he was not to visit until several years later. Rome for Byron was "the city of the soul," Venice the "home of all the pleasures, earth's paradise." Only the *signorina* could rival the *señorita*. Venice was also a city of crime and cruelty, vice and debauchery (*The Two Foscani, Marino Faliero*) and Musset, fascinated by this side of Venice as well, will also rhyme *Italie* with *amollie*.

· Musset's interest in exotic local color was not very keen, especially when compared to that of his fellow romantics. Italy is evoked by a brief reference to a gondola here or a silken ladder there, Spain by a *mantilla* or a *basquiña*. Musset was never converted to Hugo's insistence upon profuse detail "stolen" (*Namouna*) from libraries. Foreign words are used sparingly and more for instant atmosphere and bravado than for true local color. The prevailing atmosphere of the *Contes* is not that of the documentary but of fantasy—"adult fairy tales" one critic has called them.

While not keenly interested in local color, Musset *was* interested in bright vivid colors. The *Contes*, following the program of early romanticism, abound in adjectives of color, which often follow each other in embarrassing propinquity.

> Assez dormir, ma belle!
> Ta cavale isabelle
> Hennit sous tes balcons.
> Vois tes piqueurs alertes,
> Et sur leurs manches vertes
> Les pieds noirs des faucons.
> ("Le Lever")

In the seventeenth century, as Emmanuel Barat reminds us, eyes were not blue, green or black, they were *admirables*; a landscape was adequately described when called *agréable*. The adjective of color was an important part of the romantic program to bring back the *mot juste* and a more realistic and concrete vocabulary into poetic diction. Musset's skies are blue as often as they are *d'azur*, his grass green oftener than *d'émeraude*; ribbons are black, balconies gold, fringes crimson; Musset's Venice, as in some of Turner's paintings, is a violent red.

A few years later, Musset will poke fun not only at Hugo and other romantics but at his own first manner for this abuse of adjectives of color.

> Si, d'un coup de pinceau, je vous avais bâti
> Quelque ville aux toits *bleus*, quelque *blanche* mosquée,
> Quelque tirade en vers d'*or* et d'*argent* plaquée,
> Quelque description de minarets flanquée,
> Avec l'horizon *rouge* et le ciel assorti,

N'auriez-vous répondu: "Vous en avez menti."
(*Namouna*)

*
* *

The heroines of the *Contes* are conventional figures, providing atmosphere and plot more than psychological studies. They are the product not only of type casting but of type coloring: Mediterranean types with jet black hair set off by dazzlingly white skin, "sparkling" breasts. They are passionate of course and, when provoked, dangerous.

> Sourcils noirs, blanches mains; et pour la petitesse
> De ses pieds, elle était Andalouse, et comtesse.
>
> . . .
>
> Sous la tresse d'ébène on dirait, à la voir,
> Une jeune guerrière avec un casque noir.
> ("Une Andalouse")

Around them swarm romantic and melodramatic intrigues of infidelity, jealousy, revenge and death.

Musset's heroes are more interesting than his heroines, mainly because they are variants of an important literary type: the romantic hero. Despite the prevailing atmosphere of fantasy (even the tales of murder and revenge suggest at times parodies of melodrama and self-parody) the male protagonists provide the *Contes* with serious implications that are never fully developed. Don Paez is the dashing romantic hero (shown in one scene throwing a cloak over his blond moustache and jangling his golden spurs). He is the epitome of Musset's ideal: the hot-blooded *jouvenceau* at the height of his physical and sexual prowess.

> Oh! dans cette saison, de verdure et de force,
> Où la chaude jeunesse, arbre à rude écorce,
> Couvre tout de son ombre, horizon et chemin,
> Heureux, heureux, celui qui frappe de la main
> Le col d'un étalon rétif ou qui caresse
> Les seins étincelants d'une folle maîtresse!

In *Don Paez* and *Portia*, as opposed to the shorter pieces that follow, physical love is taken seriously and described lyrically in several realistic passages. It is presented as deep passion and not as recreational sex. The tragic story of *Don Paez* inspires a short digression in which the narrator-author utters a violent imprecation.

> Amour, fléau du monde, exécrable folie,
> Toi qu'un lien si frêle à la volupté lie,
> Quand par tant d'autres noeuds tu tiens à la douleur,
> Si jamais, par les yeux d'une femme sans coeur,
> Tu peux m'entrer au ventre et m'empoisonner l'âme,
> Ainsi que d'une plaie on arrache une lame,
> Plutôt que comme un lâche on me voie en souffrir,
> Je t'en arracherai, quand j'en devrais mourir.

Rafaël, of *Les Marrons du feu*, is a Byronic hero in the Don Juan mould: flippant, callous, cadish. Love to him is a short-lived affair that leads inevitably to boredom. He is the first of Musset's anti-heroes. From the beginning of the poem to the end he is identified with the clown. We first see him carrying a broken guitar and wearing a wet and tattered coat. The clown topos is made explicit in scene 2 when Rafaël presents La Camargo with a fan which, he says, is the very portrait of himself: among other things it is covered with the silver spangles of Harlequin. This motif is echoed later in a song that Rafaël sings of Trivelin and Scaramouche and more significantly at the end of the poem when the dying hero's last request is that all his worldly goods be bequeathed to his jester, Bippo. Rafaël's self-image is that of a buffoon.

> On me nomme seigneur Vide-Bourse, casseur
> De pots; c'est en anglais, Blockhead, maître tueur d'abbés.
>   . . .
> Que voulez-vous? moi j'ai donné ma vie
> A ce dieu fainéant, qu'on nomme fantaisie.
> C'est lui, qui triste ou fol, de face ou de profil,
> Comme un polichinel me traîne au bout d'un fil.

He does not try to hide a sense of emptiness. He calls himself "une cervelle sans fond" and says that he is "plus vain que la fumée/De ma pipe." He is a hollow man, emptier than a tin soldier, as a later hero, Lorenzaccio, will describe himself.

We are dealing here with a modern type of anti-hero: the sad clown endowed with (or beset by) self-consciousness—the clown who *knows* he's a clown. Rafaël's clowning not only expresses his feelings of self-worth but also serves, like the great amount of alcohol he consumes, to drown his sorrow.

> Quant à mélancolie, elle sent trop les trous
> Aux bas, le quatrième étage, et les vieux sous.
> On dit qu'elle a des gens qui se noient pour elle.
> —Moi, je la noie.

The hero of *Portia*, Dalti, is Musset's first *beau ténébreux*, a young but somber and mysterious *étranger* (the word is used four times) whose black *manteau de deuil* is matched by a black plume. He is, like Hernani (and *before* Hernani) *l'homme fatal*, doomed to misfortune and spreading misfortune around him involuntarily.

> Cette fleur avait mis dix-huit ans à s'ouvrir.
> A-t-elle pu tomber et se faner si vite,
> Pour avoir une nuit touché ma main maudite?

Dalti's tortured spirit is the result not only of his sense of doom but his loss of religious faith: he enters a church "without respect. . . but without scorn." Not without metaphysical anguish however: He cannot share his mistress's belief in everlasting happiness.

> Songez bien que tous deux
> Avant qu'il soit long-tems nous allons être vieux.
> Que je mourrai peut-être avant vous.
>
> —Dieu rassemble
> Les amans, dit Portia; nous partirons ensemble.
> Ton ange en t'emportant me prendra dans ses bras.
>
> Mais le pêcheur se tut, car il ne croyait pas.

Mardoche was appended to the *Contes* to give the volume suitable length for publication. The setting is no longer exotic but laid in contemporary Paris. It is a lively, deliberately disjointed and humorous narrative that pokes fun at certain aspects of romanticism (including anglophilia, melancholy and the macabre of "bas romantisme") and treats its hero (who, for instance, sprains his ankle while escaping from an enraged husband) with the same disrespect.

Despite the poem's comic tonality, there are serious undertones that the poet might have developed more fully. For example, the theme of love's evanescence—one of the major themes of Musset's opus and already an important leitmotif in the *Contes*—appears in *Mardoche* although presented in a light-hearted vein.

> Mais tout s'use.
> Une lune de miel n'a pas trente quartiers,
> Comme un baron saxon. —Et gare les derniers!
> L'amour (hélas! l'étrange et la fausse nature!)
> Vit d'inanition, et meurt de nourriture.
>
> Et puis, que faire? Un jour, c'est bien long. —Et demain?
> Et toujours? —L'ennui gagne. —A quoi rêver au bain?

But the reader of the *Contes* is aware of having encountered this theme repeatedly in earlier pieces and in more serious contexts. The theme is used again as the finale. Mardoche's beloved Rosine is sent to a convent. His reaction?

> Et que fit Mardoche? —Pour changer
> D'amour, il lui fallut six mois à voyager.

Mardoche's cynical *désinvolture* is given a serious explanation in a passage at the beginning of the poem.

> Peut-être que n'ayant pour se désennuyer
> Qu'un livre (c'est le coeur humain que je veux dire),
> Il avait su trop tôt, et trop avant y lire;
> C'est un grand mal d'avoir un esprit trop hâtif. . .

Mardoche is Musset's first presentation of a basic type of romantic hero who will become prominent in his work, the *puer senex*, the disillusioned and cynical young man who is old before his time.[3]

While lacking the serious side of romantic irony, the poem displays various devices that will be used to produce this new type of irony. First, *interventionnisme*: the narrative is constantly interrupted by apostrophes to the reader that inform the latter about the author's intentions and techniques; for example, not only will the poet abridge an episode, he will inform the reader of the abridgment.

> Je n'ai dessein, lecteur, de faire aucunement
> Ici, ce qu'à Paris l'on appelle un roman.
> Peu s'en faut qu'un auteur, qui pas à pas chemine,
> Ne vous fasse coucher avec son héroïne.
> Ce n'est pas ma manière; et, si vous permettez,
> Ce sera quinze jours que nous aurons sautés.

Then there is the mock-heroic tonality.

> O bois silencieux! ô lacs!— O murs gardés!
> Balcons quittés si tard! si vite escaladés!
>
> . . .
>
> Et toi, lampe d'argent, pâle et fraîche lumière
> Qui fais les douces nuits plus blanches que le lait!
> —Soutenez mon haleine en ce divin couplet!
>
> Je veux chanter ce jour d'éternelle mémoire
> Où, son dîner fini, devant qu'il fit nuit noire,
> Notre héros, le nez caché sous son manteau
> Monta dans sa voiture une heure au moins trop tôt!

8

The poet will even poke fun at his own poem by pointing out, in a rhymed note, the weakness of the plot's ending.

> Cette fin est usée; et nous la donnons telle,
> Par grand éloignement de la mode nouvelle.

It is clear that the narrator does not take very seriously what he is narrating.

In *Namouna* such devices will be used not just for one-dimensional humor as here but to produce a tonality of ambivalence. *Mardoche* is charming but thin; *Namouna* will give off more meaningful vibrations.

One of the most salient features of the narrative poems is their swiftness. The narrator moves so quickly from one episode to another that intermediary but important ones are sometimes omitted. Musset's use of narrative ellipsis often creates suspense or mystery but also unintentional obscurity at times (see S. Jeune, "Aspects" p. 180). The dialogues and descriptions are also rapid-fire affairs. Musset is basically a synecdochist: there are no full-length portraits of his heroes and heroines, no lengthy narrative or scenic passages, only flashes of action or colors (primary colors especially). In *Don Paez* for example, a soldier becomes simply "une moustache rousse;" a beautiful girl passes by, "blanche avec un oeil noir;" a "yellow and blue dragoon" sleeps in the hay. And Mardoche, who casts his cloak "over his blond moustache,"

> . . . avait pour voisine
> Deux yeux napolitains qui s'appelaient Rosine.

In *Portia* the duelists are transformed by synecdoche into a cinematographic close-up: "deux lames qui brillent et qui se heurtent." In a later work, *Louison*, three women at a masked ball are reduced by synecdoche to "trois morceaux de carton jasant sous leurs dentelles." As mentioned earlier, Musset displays considerable (or relative) restraint as a local colorist, constantly presenting the part for the whole. A silken ladder and a balcony are the only props in one scene, a mantilla the only costume in another. Here too we see a synecdochist at work.

*
* *

The long dramatic and narrative poems are followed by several brief and often short-syllabled "Songs to be set to Music," evoking mainly Spanish and Italian atmosphere but having no pretentions to being anything more than what they are: sprightly serenades. "L'Andalouse" presents the conventional Spanish maiden of romantic lore—

Avez-vous vu, dans Barcelone,
Une Andalouse au sein bruni?
Pâle comme un beau soir d'automne!

   . . .

Sa chevelure qui l'inonde,
Plus longue qu'un manteau de roi.

   . . .

Et sa basquiña sur sa hanche. . .

Also romantic are the touches of realism, the *seins brunis* (reduced by a conventional synecdoche to the singular) of the first stanza, the *seins nus* of the sixth, and the famous epithet, "ma lionne!" (In "Madrid" the mistress is called "un vrai démon" as well as the conventional *ange*—and in the same line, creating an antithesis warmly applauded by the Cénacle; and when making love she is compared to an agile adder.)

The love evoked in the shorter pieces of the *Contes* is lighthearted and superficial, on the thematic lines of "Assez dormir, ma belle" ("Le lever") or this:

Or si d'aventure on s'enquête
Qui m'a valu telle conquête,
C'est l'allure de mon cheval,
Un compliment sur sa mantille,
Puis des bonbons à la vanille
Par un beau soir de carnaval.
   ("Madrid")

However, in the middle of "Madame la Marquise" a new note appears, the mood of the joyous reveler suddenly turns sour: he reveals his "longue détresse."

Oh! viens dans mon âme froissée,
Qui saigne encor d'un mal bien grand.

   . . .

Car sais-tu seulement, pour vivre,
Combien il m'a fallu pleurer?
De cet ennui qui désenivre,
Combien en mon coeur dévorer?

This is the first personal note in Musset's hitherto impersonal poetry and introduces what will become one of the major themes of his work: bitterness inspired by the betrayal of a mistress. But his mood, just as quickly, changes back to flippant good humor. These sudden changes of mood will become one of the marks of his style.

The serious mood surfaces again in the three pieces that follow. In

"A Madame X. . ." Musset alludes once again to the first betrayal of his young love-life:

> A tes pièges d'un jour on ne me prendra plus.

In "Au Jung-Frau" the poet indulges in elaborate praise: He hints at having met "a heart" so sublime and pure (it is compared hyperbolically to the majestic mountain) as to be inaccessible to mere mortal man. In "A Ulric G." he envies the profound grief of an older, more experienced friend unhappy in love. In another hyperbole, rather rare for Musset, the depth of his friend's "limitless" grief is compared to that of the sea.

"Venise" presents once again the gay mood and musical qualities of the *Chanson*. As he frequently did in the narrative poems, and as he will continue to do throughout his poetic career, Musset uses imagery to animate the inanimate. Boats for instance—

> Autour de lui, par groupes,
> Navires et chaloupes,
> Pareils à des hérons
>   Couchés en ronds,
> Dorment sur l'eau qui fume. . .

and the moon—

> La lune qui s'efface
> Couvre son front qui passe
> D'un nuage étoilé
>   Demi voilé.

> Ainsi, la dame abbesse
> De Sainte-Croix rabaisse
> Sa cape aux larges plis
>   Sur son surplis.

With "Stances," another descriptive poem, we move from "Venice the red" to the brooding grey ruins of a gothic monastery in the Pyrenees set off by two romantic motifs—a desolate valley and a violent autumnal lightening storm.

In "Sonnet" Musset proves himself to be a master of a genre seldom practiced by other romantics. The sonnet ends with a surprise, from apparently neutral description to a personal note—a switch that is already becoming familiar to Musset's readers. The sonnet will be analyzed in detail in chapter five.

With the famous "Ballade à la lune" Musset experiments not only with an irregular ballad form (quatrains rather than *dizains*, and vers *hétérométriques*: 6,6,2,6) but especially with parody—first of all parody of the ballad form itself. The poem shocked not only the neo-classicists but many romantics as well. The poet pokes fun at the stereotyped feelings and pseudo-feelings inspired by the moon and also the contemporary abuse of adjectives of color by early romantics (like himself).

> C'était, dans la nuit brune,
> Sur le clocher jauni,
>   La lune,
> Comme un point sur un i.

In a conclusion omitted form the 1830 edition Musset's irreverent attitude toward the moon takes on a Byronic touch of naughtiness.

> Le pied dans sa pantoufle,
> Voilà l'époux tout prêt
>   Qui souffle
> Le bougeoir indiscret.
>
> Au pudique hyménée
> La vierge qui se croit
>   Menée,
> Grelotte en son lit froid,
>
> Mais monsieur tout en flamme
> Commence à rudoyer
> Madame,
> Qui commence à crier.
>
> "Ouf! dit-il, je travaille,
> Ma bonne, et ne fais rien
>   Qui vaille;
> Tu ne te tiens pas bien."
>
> Et vite il se dépêche.
> Mais quel démon caché.
>   L'empêche
> De commettre un péché?

The culprit is the inquisitive moon. The audacious simile that opens and closes the poem would have been better received in our own century than in Musset's. At the end of the nineteenth century Laforgue too will speak irreverently of the moon but with an ironic ambivalence that is missing here. Why Musset's delightfully fresh imagery did not delight all his contemporaries is hard to imagine, at least from hindsight.

N'es-tu qu'une boule?
Qu'un grand faucheux bien gras
Qui roule sans pattes et sans bras?

. . .

Qui t'avait éborgnée
L'autre nuit? T'étais-tu
Cognée
A quelque arbre pointu?

Musset carries ironic deflation to its extreme: La Fontaine's noble periphrasis for the sun, "l'oeil de la nature," becomes the burlesque *oeil borgne* and the demythologized moon even becomes a daddy-long-legs without legs!

*
* *

Musset's versification in the *Contes* exhibits the romantic determination to make the rigid alexandrine of the preceding two centuries more supple. The *trimètre*, the displaced caesura and enjambement are used frequently; sometimes all three are used in the same line.

Une femme pieds nus, decouverte à moitié,
Gisait.—C'était horreur de la voir. —Et pitié.
(*Don Paez*)

Enjambement becomes deliberately outrageous in *Mardoche* where more than one sentence is forced to straddle two stanzas, and where a line can end with the slightest of grammatical tool-words:

Il n'avait vu ni Kean, ni Bonaparte, ni

anticipating, by the way, a mannerism of contemporary poetry, the ending of a line with *d'*.

The *Contes* also reveal Musset's early interest in rich rhyme and in rhythmical virtuosity.

Que j'aime à voir, dans la vallée
Désolée
Se lever comme mausolée
Les quatre ailes d'un noir moutier!
Que j'aime à voir, près de l'austère
Monastère,
Au seuil du baron feudataire,
La croix blanche et le bénitier!
("Stances")

In the same poem "gothiques" rhymes richly with "portiques" and "athlétiques." Musset soon tired of the frantic search for rich rhymes and deliberately weakened some of them even before the publication of the first edition. A statistical analysis has shown that throughout Musset's entire opus forty-eight per cent of his rhymes are not even *suffisantes*, because they are homologous, or because the pretonic syllables are too similar, or because a long vowel is rhymed with a short one.[4]

Musset also carried forward the romantic revolution in poetic diction. He joined Hugo and other romantics in seeking the *mot propre* (sometimes, even, the *mot gras*) and in attacking the ornamental periphrasis and epithet and the noble synonym—although his own work is never thoroughly rid of them. Deliberately violating classical canons of good taste, he will label one of his heroines, as we have seen, with the bold epithet "ma lionne!;" her complexion is described by an even bolder simile: "Elle est jaune comme une orange." Rafaël of the *Marrons du feu* describes himself as "salé comme un hareng!" La Camargo feels like "un vieux soulier." In his dialogues Musset strives for realism and is adept at portraying the idiom of coquettes and dandies, of quarrelling soldiers and jilted lovers, brooding misanthropes, gay débauchés, insouciant libertines. He is not afraid of committing a hiatus

> Aujourd'hui est à nous.
> (*Marrons*)

or a solecism

> C'est quand on dit d'un homme
> Qu'il est jaloux. Ceux-là, c'est ainsi qu'on les nomme.
> (*Portia*)

or an anacoluthon

> Car, j'en sais par le monde
> Que jamais ni brune ni blonde
> N'ont valu le bout de son doigt.
> ("Madrid")

While the *Contes* abound in literal images, the volume is not particularly dense in imagery of the figurative type. By my count 8 per cent of the 500 lines of *Don Paez* contain metaphors or similes. The 31 similes outnumber the metaphors 4 to 1 and a couple of them are clichés ("brune comme un jais;" "plus prompt qu'une flèche") which could be subtracted from the total. Musset's similes are generally traditional, but he does manage to refresh clichés through slight changes in wording or rhythm (see Rolande Berteau, "Procédes de revivification. . .," pp. 39-46). Figures other than metaphor, simile and synecdoche are rare: a few transferred epithets, 3 metonymies (of which 2 are clichés) 2 examples each of syllepsis (e.g., "Et laissez vos regards avec le vin couler.") and oxymoron.

The most striking tropes are of the extended, Homeric type.

> Comme on voit dans l'été, sur les herbes fauchées,
> Deux louves, remuant les feuilles déssechées,
> S'arrêter face à face, et se montrer la dent;
> La rage les excite au combat; cependant
> Elles tournent en rond lentement, et s'attendent;
> Leurs mufles amaigris l'un vers l'autre se tendent.
> Tels, et se renvoyant de plus sombres regards,
> Les deux rivaux, penchés sur le bord des remparts,
> S'observent. . .
> (Don Paez)

The density of imagery does not increase in the poems that follow *Don Paez*. In *Les Marrons* and *Portia* less than 5 per cent of the lines contain metaphors or similes (in *Mardoche* less than 3 per cent) and the ratio between them remains 4 to 1.

Throughout his opus Musset uses the girl=flower image with disconcerting frequency but usually, as in *Portia*, the cliché is rejuvenated through amplification.

> O nature, nature!
> Murmura l'étranger, —vois cette créature;
> Sous les cieux les plus doux qui la pouvaient nourrir,
> Cette fleur avait mis dix-huit ans à s'ouvrir.
> A-t-elle pu tomber et se faner si vite,
> Pour avoir une nuit touché ma main maudite?
> . . .
> Avait-elle hésité? — Je ne sais; —mais bientôt,
> Comme une tendre fleur que le vent déracine,
> Faible, et qui lentement sur sa tige s'incline,
> Telle, elle détourna la tête, et lentement
> S'inclina toute en pleurs jusqu'à son jeune amant.

While this city-dweller can in no way be classified as a nature poet, nature is the predominant source of his imagery. A bright-colored fan is compared to a peacock; so is a *grisette*. An Andalousian beauty is as pale as a fine autumn evening. La Camargo, enraged by jealousy, is compared to a raven attracted to a corpse. Beautiful women are compared not only to the inevitable and ubiquitous flowers but also to birds, fawns, clinging ivy, heifers, limpid streams; their supple figures are compared to reeds and swaying palm trees. This tendency to use nature as the vehicle for a simile will continue throughout his work.

> Un bourgeon vert à côté d'elle
> Se balançait sur l'arbrisseau;
> Je vis poindre une fleur nouvelle;
> La plus jeune était la plus belle:
> L'homme est ainsi, toujours nouveau.
> (*La Nuit d'Août*)

Rarely does Musset reverse the direction and make nature the tenor of an image for which the vehicle is a human being. When manufactured objects are used as vehicles, they are usually negative in denotation, connotation or symbolic value. La Camargo's jealous love is compared to a twisted sword blade that cannot be removed from the heart without breaking the soul; if her love is spurned, she will feel as abandoned "as an old shoe that no longer serves any purpose." A faithless woman is made of that false metal used to mint counterfeit coins.

One of the most persistent stylistic traits, not only in the *Contes* but throughout the opus, is the personification of abstractions. Hatred is compared to a poisoner; old age is portrayed as an invincible giant; Dalti's tragic fate is described in terms of an impoverished prostitute decked out for a carnival. In *Mardoche* the frenzied joy of a successful lover is personified as a servant placing a crown on the hero's head, a robe of purple on his shoulders.

Despite their obvious romantic features, the *Contes* stand apart as an original creation. The poems are bolder than what the romantic program called for in the areas of enjambement and rhythmic virtuosity, tamer in the areas of rich rhyme and local color. The wit, verve and flippancy were a departure from the high seriousness of fellow romantics who were soon to develop the dogma of the poet as prophet, seer and leader of mankind. Although Hugo was developing his *mélange des genres* for the romantic theater at this time, Musset's abrupt shifts in tone can be found nowhere among his contemporaries except occasionally in Mérimée and later in the prose of some minor romantics like Pétrus Borel. Nowhere in the *Contes* can one find brooding melancholy, and Nature is played down by this poet of the city. Musset uses with restraint what his colleagues were abusing: descriptive and exotic detail, antithesis, hyperbole and melodrama. His flirtation with adjectives of color was brief and was the

16

object of self-parody within the *Contes* themselves. Even the Byronic tonality of the *Contes* has an original flavor; if it had not yet existed, Musset would certainly have invented it. He did not simply borrow the style of *Don Juan*, he adapted it to his own purposes and presented the reader with a similar but still unique implied author. To be sure, we see the proud aristocrat and dandy, the young sensualist who yearns for love both passionately and mistrustingly, the casual, nonchalant and witty conversationalist (which the real Musset was not, but the way); but there is no sign of Byron's passion for nature and politics, and none of his bitterness and misanthropy can be found in Musset's irony. At a time when melancholy was in great favor as a literary theme, Musset dared poke fun at it.

> Quant à mélancolie, elle sent trop les trous
> Aux bas, le quatrième étage, et les vieux sous.
> (*Marrons*)

We see, rather, a kind of cheerful cynicism, which was not a pose but the fruit of the poet's still limited experience and still developing personality. Another distinguishing trait is an optimism that implies that life is definitely worth living (at least until the age of thirty). It is especially Musset's irony that sets him apart from his peers in France, the kind of irony that suggests that his narrator does not fully believe the stories he is telling us.

Technically, the *Contes* must be considered a triumph, especially for a nineteen-year-old poet who has already mastered most of the tricks of the trade. Musset moves with equal ease in the long dramatic narrative, the short song and sonnet, the oversized ballad, the medieval *aubade*. His plots are fast moving and always achieve an ascending gradation of interest. His descriptions, while short and sober, are suggestive, and he has been rightly praised as a miniaturist. His dialogues are distinguished by their naturalness, his narratives by their vivid realism and appropriate imagery. He shares with other romantic poets the ability to bring life to inanimate objects. The limitations of the *Contes* are the limitations of the genre itself. We are dealing with a poetry of fantasy, not of subtle emotions or deep thoughts. Serious ideas are present, more implicit than explicit, but the genre dictates that they be presented swiftly or framed with ironic detachment.

chapter two
AFTER 1830: A POET OF
MANY STYLES AND GENRES

Musset's first manner was only that—his first. In a letter dated January 1830 he writes: "Je suis loin d'avoir une manière arrêtée. J'en changerai probablement plusieurs fois encore" (*Correspondance*, p. 24). This does not mean, however, that he will forever abandon the flamboyant romanticism of the *Contes*.

> Ils disent tous que je suis converti, converti à quoi? S'imaginent-ils que, je me suis confessé à l'abbé Delisle ou que j'ai été frappé de la grâce en lisant Laharpe? On s'attend sans doute à ce que, au lieu de dire: "Prends ton épée et tue-le", je dirai désormais: "Arme ton bras d'un glaive homicide et tranche le fil de ses jours." Bagatelle pour bagatelle, j'aimerais encore mieux recommencer *Les Marrons du feu* et *Mardoche*. (Ibid., p. 28)

The goal of this chapter is a modest one: to acquaint the reader with the wide variety of genres and styles the poet attempted from 1830 to the end of his relatively short career. A discussion of Musset's poetics and of his imaginative universe is reserved for the two chapters that follow, and detailed stylistic analyses of several key poems will be found in the chapters of Part Two.

*
* *

1. Shorter Poems

Musset's shorter pieces are written in many different genres: elegy, sonnet, rondeau, madrigal, *chanson*, romance, ballad, epigram, epistle, *billet*, *impromptu*. Some, like "Un Rêve," his first published poem, and "Une Vision," another early work, deal with the fantastic; others (e.g., "Charles-Quint," Jeanne d'Arc," "Napoléon") with the historical. They offer a wide variety of moods, from the very grave ("Sur la Naissance du Conte de Paris") to the light and humorous ("Le Songe du Reviewer"). The theological seriousness of the long poem *L'Espoir en Dieu* was immediately followed by the brief and frivolous "A la mi-Carême," showing, as his brother Paul tells us, the "mobility" of a young and impressionable mind. Stylistically, the shorter pieces are characterized on the whole by a simplicity that contrasts sharply with the flamboyant manner of the *Contes*. The vocabulary is ordinary, there are few learned allusions and few bold images. A sustained repetition here and there is the only rhetorical device consistently used. Many poems are little more than rhymed prose. Many others are quite charming or witty: Musset was the only major French romantic poet with a sustained sense of humor.

From the point of view of versification, these shorter pieces reveal that Musset has given up his romantic taste for experimentation. The most notable feature is the frequent use of *vers mêlés*. In "Adieu" the octosyllable is used with the decasyllable; in "Rappelle-toi" the decasyllable is used with the alexandrine as well as with lines of 6 and 4 syllables. In some pieces the length of a line is just half that of the preceding one: 8+4 in "Mimi Pinson" and "Adieux à Suzon," 10+5 in "Conseils à une Parisienne." The uneven line is occasionally used: seven syllables in "Le Rideau de ma voisine," for instance, and five syllables in "La Nuit."

A good number of the shorter pieces, as one would expect, are merely occasional poetry—tokens of thanks, fits of pique, etc. Most of the *épîtres* are addressed to friends, mistresses, ex-mistresses and would-be mistresses. The most noteworthy of these deal with the various forms and stages of love and friendship. Several pieces ("A Pépa," "A Juana," "A Ninon," "A Aimée d'Alton") express a charming, superficial infatuation, usually in an unaffected tone and unmannered idiom.

> Quand le sommeil sur ta famille
> Autour de toi s'est répandu,
> O Pépita, charmante fille,
> Mon amour, à quoi penses-tu?

Qui sait? Peut-être à l'héroïne
De quelque infortuné roman:
A tout ce que l'espoir devine
Et la réalité dément;

Peut-être à ces grandes montagnes
Qui n'accouchent que de souris;
A des amoureux en Espagne,
A des bonbons, à des maris;

Peut-être aux tendres confidences
D'un coeur naïf comme le tien;
A ta robe, aux airs que tu danses;
Peut-être à moi, —peut-être à rien.

("A Pépa")

The tone changes with the George Sand cycle, seven short pieces written between August 1833 and January 1835, published posthumously, and which belong to the mainstream of the serious love lyric. The first poem celebrates the triumphant return of love to a heart that for three years had thought itself cured and hardened. In another the poet contrasts true love and the true happiness it brings with the vain "comédie humaine." But the last three pieces record the end of the stormy love affair.

Il faudra bien t'y faire à cette solitude,
Pauvre coeur insensé, tout prêt à se rouvrir,
Qui sait si mal aimer et sait si bien souffrir.
("A George Sand" V)

Et cet amour si doux, qui faisait sur la vie
Glisser dans un baiser nos deux coeurs confondus,
Toi qui me l'as appris, tu ne t'en souviens plus.
("A George Sand" VI)

To the woman who thus not only rejected the poet's love but erased the happy times from her memory the final piece sends a desperate plea for remembrance.

Fais riche un autre amour et souviens-toi du mien.
Laisse mon souvenir te suivre loin de France;
Qu'il parte sur ton coeur, pauvre bouquet fané,
Lorsque tu l'as cueilli, j'ai connu l'Espérance,
Je croyais au bonheur, et toute ma souffrance
Est de l'avoir perdu sans te l'avoir donné.
("A George Sand" VII)

The cycle is noteworthy for its sober tonality which prevents the frequent rhetorical devices (apostrophe, hyperbole, personification, anaphora and the ornamental epithet) from weakening the convincing expression of genuine love and genuine sorrow.

Vladimir Nabokov has said that French romanticism has given us the poetry of love and German romanticism the poetry of friendship. But Musset is a poet for whom friendship too was important both personally and poetically: A good proportion of his opus is addressed to close friends and near-friends. In "A Ulric G." and "A mon ami Edouard B", for example, he commiserates with two friends who have suffered disappointments in love. He envies the former for his "blessure" and his "maux;" to the latter he expresses a romantic aesthetics:

> Ah! frappe-toi le coeur, c'est là qu'est le génie.
> C'est là qu'est la pitié, la souffrance et l'amour.

In "A mon ami Alfred T." Musset praises Alfred Tatet for not being a fair weather friend, for staying with him through adversity; the theme then develops into that of pain, just as it was for love, being the true measure of friendship.

> Mais du moins j'aurais pu, frère, quoi qu'il m'arrive,
> De mon cachet de deuil sceller notre amitié,
> Et, que demain je meure ou que demain je vive,
> Pendant que mon coeur bat, t'en donner la moitié.

In another poem addressed to Tatet, Musset celebrates the sybaritic pleasures of youth and the more lasting joys of friendship.

> —Oui, la vie est un bien, la joie est une ivresse;
> Il est doux d'en user sans crainte et sans soucis;
> Il est doux de fêter les dieux de la jeunesse,
> De couronner de fleurs son verre et sa maîtresse,
> D'avoir trente ans comme Dieu l'a permis.
> Et, si jeunes encore, d'être de vieux amis.

For Victor Hugo Musset entones a ringing tribute to friendship winning out over a literary quarrel. To Charles Nodier he expresses, years later, his nostalgia for the friendship of the Cénacle days. To his brother Paul returning from Italy he expresses with touching sincerity his deep affection.

> Ami, ne t'en va plus si loin.
> D'un peu d'aide j'ai grand besoin.
>   Quoi qu'il m'advienne,

> Je ne sais où va mon chemin,
> Mais je marche mieux quand ma main
>   Serre la tienne.

Of the other short pieces the most successful are the *chansons* and the sonnets, the former for their often Verlaine-like musicality (a topic to be discussed at length in chapter 8), the later for their formal perfection (one of which will be analyzed in chapter 5). Partly because of the flexibility of his rhyme schemes and partly because of his natural talent, there is never any feeling of strain in the sonnets. Their moods range from extreme joy ("Qu'il est doux d'être au monde...") to extreme sorrow, that for example, of the well known "Tristesse."

> J'ai perdu ma force et ma vie,
> Et mes amis et ma gaieté;
> J'ai perdu jusqu'à la fierté
> Qui faisait croire à mon génie.
>
>   . . .
>
> Le seul bien qui me reste au monde
> Est d'avoir quelquefois pleuré.

*
* *

2. *Narrative Poetry*

During the still formative years that followed the publication of the *Contes*, Musset was groping for a style of narrative poetry that would be truly his own, in the sense of being in accord with his temperament and in the sense of finding his unique voice. *Suzon* and *Octave*, both written in 1831, continue the flippant Byronic manner and the Italo-Hispanic atmosphere of the *Contes*. They are minor works and hastily written, as evidenced by the somewhat confused plots and the sloppy versification (some lines do not even have a rhyme). *Suzon* is a licentious and sacrilegious tale of two debauched and atheistic priests who stop at nothing, including murder, to seduce an unwilling woman. *Octave*, as a drama of jealousy and vengeance, does not represent an advance in the quality of Musset's writing, it is in fact inferior to *Portia* and to *Don Paez*.

It was also during this early period that Musset wrote most of the long "fragment," *Le Saule*, which marks a new poetic manner in its great length, its sustained seriousness and its oratorical style. The piece abounds in apostrophes, ornamental periphrases, rhetorical questions, personification of abstractions and classical clichés like "le manteau de la nuit." The tale is basically a melodrama in which Georgette, the idealized herione, is sent off to a convent by her father to protect her chastity from the advances of the young Tiburce. (Tiburce is a composite of several types of romantic hero: He has the blond hair and delicate, "effeminate" features of the author himself; his eyes however have the hardness and severity of the Byronic hero; like many another romantic hero, he was born in poverty and is an orphan; like Coelio of *Les Caprices de Marianne*, his voice is sad, and like Coelio again, Tiburce is the bookish, studious type; like Manfred and Faust he is a solitary seeker of Life's mystery but soon discovers that human knowledge is vanity.) Georgette languishes in the absence of her lover, who finally arrives, disguised as a monk. But too late: she dies of grief and he in turn will die by his own hand.

The two most famous passages are the invocation to the Evening Star and the Hymn to the Sun, which are not directly related to the narrative. Some critics have exclaimed over these "morceaux choisis;" others have complained of "passages passe-partout." One critic (Maurice Grammont) has shown that they are "suggestively" related to the plot and theme. In any event we are at the farthest remove from the casual style of *Mardoche*.

Pâle étoile du soir, messagère lointaine,
Dont le front sort brillant des voiles du couchant,
De ton palais d'azur, au sein du firmament,
   Que regardes-tu dans la plaine?

Etoile, où t'en vas-tu, dans cette nuit immense?
Cherches-tu sur la rive un lit dans les roseaux?
Ou t'en vas-tu, si belle, à l'heure du silence,
   Tomber comme une perle au sein profond des eaux?

Ah! si tu dois mourir, bel astre, et si ta tête
Va dans la vaste mer plonger ses blonds cheveux,
Avant de nous quitter, un seul instant arrête; —
   Etoile de l'amour, ne descends pas des cieux!

Namouna was originally intended as a filler to add volume to the first "livraison" of *Un Spectacle dans un fauteuil*. The poem is an ironic treatment of the Don Juan myth. There are in fact two Don Juans here: the idealized hero of the second canto and Hassan, the cynical hero of the first and final cantos. The latter is a cheerful débauché with a repressed *Weltschmerz*, a creature of paradox and ambivalence. The two Don Juan types are an expression of Musset's contradictory personality and of his contradictory attitudes toward love. Despite the basically comic presentation, the poem treats obliquely of the poet's disarray: One senses tears at times behind the laughter, "signals of a heart of pain," as Pushkin said of the "motley" chapters of his half-sad, half-mirthful *Eugene Onegin*. And the poem's romantic irony makes it denser than a cursory reading would suggest. This new form of irony found in *Namouna* will be analyzed in chapter 6.

Musset's most important narrative poem is *Rolla*. The story is well known. The hero is a young nobleman whom an improvident father has left with a modest inheritance which must last Rolla a lifetime since he has too much aristocratic pride to consider assuming a profession or learning a trade. He abhors the habits and routine of everyday life and looks with misanthropic scorn upon kings and paupers alike. A romantic hero, he walks "naked and alone in this masquerade called Life." Since the future holds no promise of happiness or meaningfulness, he sets out systematically to squander his small fortune on three years of debauchery; when he is down to his last few pennies, he will spend them on a prostitute and kill himself.

On the surface Rolla is a Don Juan of the Mardoche-Hassan mould. But he possesses neither their flippancy nor their caddishness, and the poet insists on his good qualities rather than his failings. He is, for instance, "loyal, intrépide et superbe" and "naïf . . . comme l'enfance." And despite his wayward ways, his heart remains pure. *Pur* is the most important and, with its synonym, *chaste*, the most frequently used epithet in the poem; it points up the pathos of Rolla's situation. It is his nostalgia for the purity of childhood and the very vestiges of that purity that make his situation tragic. He is not a wicked young man but rather an *enfant du siècle*, that is, a victim of the philosophical disarray of his times.

The poem does not end on a note of total despair. The prostitute with whom Rolla spends his last night on earth, Marie, is even younger than he—she is 15, he 20—and her heart, like his, is still virginally pure. In Musset's casuistry the "heart" is not contaminated by the vile actions of the body: everything seems to depend on "the direction of intention." Through the long night the two young people experience, not love but "the specter of love." At the very end they do experience—if only a brief moment—the ecstasy of real love. The poem leaves the reader with the suggestion that if a new, viable Faith arose it would find ready adherents even among the cynical and degenerate youth of modern times. The suggestion is prepared by an earlier passage:

> Penses-tu cependant que si quelque croyance,
> Si le plus léger fil le retenait encor,
> Il viendrait sur ce lit prostituer sa mort?

Generically, *Rolla* is as much an ode as a narrative poem. The slender plot serves as pretext for a series of lyrical fragments, more or less directly related to it, that express in sustained oratory the philosophical implications of the story.

Rolla does not appear at all in the first canto. The narrator, who is both a persona of the poet and a kindred spirit of the hero, represents especially the youth of Musset's time. The tone is one of high seriousness; there is not a trace of irony or nonchalance here or in any of the cantos. The first movement begins with no fewer than twelve successive rhetorical questions. The first one introduces the general theme— "Do you miss the days when the gods were alive and life was young?." The eleven others serve as anaphorical (i.e., musical) amplifications. The canto ends with seven more rhetorical questions developing musically the theme "Where is there a Savior, a saint for us? Where is hope?"

A noteworthy feature of the poem's overall structure is the rapid juxtaposition of fragments, which are not linked by explicit transitional material but which do contribute to the whole. The poet passes from one fragment to another at a breathless pace, which is at times disconcerting. This aspect of Musset's style has been observed by Philippe Van Tieghem: "Musset. . . procède par raccourcis. . . Les images sont comme des hallucinations rapides, des 'illuminations' instantanées, que le poète n'a pas le temps d'expliquer, mais qui suppose toute une scène symbolique" (*Musset*, p. 61) and by Emile Montégut: "Rapide, primesautière, l'inspiration de Musset procède par bonds qui, aussi rapprochés qu'ils soient, laissent toujours entre eux un certain intervalle" (*Nos Morts*, p. 260).

The second canto finally introduces Rolla, describing him as the greatest débauché of the world's most libertine city. But an extended metaphor immediately qualifies the hyperbole.

> . . . son corps était l'hôtellerie
> Où s'étaient attablés ces pâles voyageurs;
> Tantôt pour y briser les lits et les murailles,
> Pour s'y chercher dans l'ombre, et s'ouvrir les entrailles,
> Comme des cerfs en rut et des gladiateurs;
> Tantôt pour y chanter, en s'enivrant ensemble,
> Comme de gais oiseaux qu'un coup de vent rassemble,
> Et qui, pour vingt amours, n'ont qu'un arbuste en fleurs.

Rolla is pictured here not as a man of sinful intentions but simply as a passive creature indolently watching his passions perform (cf. the simile that precedes the long metaphor: "il les [ses passions] laissait aller/Comme un pâtre assoupi regarde l'eau couler.") The image of the *hôtellerie* supports the body/heart antimony that allows Musset's hero to retain his essential purity while his body is the mere locus of unseemly actions. The passage offers an excellent example of Musset's animating imagery— passions presented as drunken, raucous travelers in a tavern—his pictorial gifts, and the appropriateness of imagery to theme, qualities that characterize most of the poet's work. The metaphor is unusual because of its length and because it is fed by two similes the latter of which is itself extended.

The rest of the second canto switches back and forth from Rolla to a series of digressions only tangentially related to the plot but which do bear on Rolla's moral and metaphysical situation. By way of contrast we move from Rolla's lack of worldly, professional and moral ambition to Hercules choosing, in a happier time, "Vertu" over "Volupté"; then we move from a one-line restatement of Rolla's dissipated life—

> Rolla fit à vingt ans ce qu'avaient fait ses pères.

26

— to an eleven-line digression on the sinfulness of large modern cities; then from Rolla's haughty pride and noble heart to the famous digression on *la cavale sauvage.*

> Lorsque dans le désert la cavale sauvage,
> Après trois jours de marche, attend un jour d'orage
> Pour boire l'eau du ciel sur les palmiers poudreux. . . .
>
> . . .
>
> Elle cherche son puits dans le désert immense.
>
> . . .
>
> Alors elle se couche, et ses grands yeux s'éteignent,
> Et le pâle désert roule sur son enfant
> Les flots silencieux de son linceul mouvant.
>
> Elle ne savait pas, lorsque les caravanes
> Avec leurs chameliers passaient sous les platanes,
>
> Qu'elle n'avait qu'à suivre et qu'à baisser le front
> Pour trouver à Bagdad de fraîches écuries.

While there is no explicit link made between the *cavale* and Rolla, implicit analogies abound: the noble race, the proud thoroughbred; the "savage," untamed nature of both horse and hero; the tragic death after three days of anguished wandering in the desert, an objective correlative of Rolla's three years of aimless and anguished wandering in the *vaste désert d'hommes* called Paris; and finally the refusal to join the herd to trade freedom for safety and comfort.

> Si Dieu nous a tirés tous de la même fange,
> Certe, il a dû pétrir dans une argile étrange
> Et sécher aux rayons d'un soleil irrité
> Cet être, quel qu'il soit, ou l'aigle, ou l'hirondelle,
> Qui ne saurait plier ni son cou ni son aile,
> Et qui n'a pour tout bien qu'un mot: la liberté.

Canto III is an ode to purity, that of childhood and early adolescence, as exemplified paradoxically by Marie, the young prostitute. It is especially while she sleeps that she retains her virginal purity: For Musset the dreams of youth are not fulfillments of repressed erotic wishes but, rather, a healthy regression back to the primordial innocence of man before the first sin. A short digression on Eve obliquely reinforces the theme.

This romantic narrative is expressed in a predominantly neo-classic style: The entire poem is studded with rhetorical questions and apostrophes; regular alexandrines prodominate; and in the main the imagery is unobtrusive and traditional (snow is paler, marble less sparkling white than the milky skin of this sleeping child, etc.)

Also interesting stylistically is the way the numerous digressions are woven musically into the narrative; they come not as simple restatements but as variations on a theme. In Canto IV for example Musset interweaves contrapuntally the passionate love-making of Rolla and Marie with equally passionate invective against Voltaire, who is used as a synecdoche for all the "démolisseurs stupides" of the Enlightenment. The counterpoint itself expresses, without the need of explicit statement, the cause and effect relationship the poet is trying to establish:

> Dors-tu content, Voltaire, et ton hideux sourire
> Voltige-t-il encor sur tes os décharnés?
>
> . . .
>
> Il est tombé sur nous, cet édifice immense
> Que de tes larges mains tu sapais nuit et jour.
>
> . . .
>
> Entends-tu soupirer ces enfants qui s'embrassent?
>
> . . .
>
> Des sanglots inouis, des plaintes oppressées,
> Ouvrent en frissonnant leurs lèvres insensées.
> En les baisant au front le Plaisir s'est pâmé.
> Regarde!— ils n'aiment pas, ils n'ont jamais aimé.

The interweaving of narrative and apostrophe is effective here, it produces density thanks to the philosophical overtones: The demise of Christianity means not only that the thirst for the ideal and the absolute will never be satisfied, but also that men have lost their faith in each other; human love is now an empty simulacrum of true love. In desperation, modern man, for whom Rolla is a symbol, replaces the ancient hope for life and joy eternal with a grudging acceptance of the ephemeral, an anguished hedonism.

*

* *

28

3. Dramatic Poetry

It was also during his early period that Musset made his theatrical debut, which was traumatically unsuccessful. *La Nuit vénitienne* (December 1, 1831) was greeted with hoots and whistles and had to be withdrawn after just two performances, partly because of a staging accident, partly because the romantics were disappointed to find that the play was a throwback to Marivaux rather than an experimental drama constructed along Hugolian lines, and partly too because the classicists had not forgiven the irreverent author of the *Contes*. Humiliated, Musset renounced the legitimate theater until as late as 1847. But he did devote his considerable dramatic gifts to the creation of an Armchair Theater, *Un Spectacle dans un fauteuil,* poetic dramas designed not for the live stage and a live audience but for readers of dramatic poetry and prose.

His first contribution to the Armchair Theater, *La Coupe et les Lèvres* (1832) is a "dramatic poem," a genre that Musset was the first to introduce into French literature and modeled on Goethe's *Faust* and Byron's *Manfred*. It is also a "tragedy" because it presents us with a tragic hero in the same sense that Goethe and Byron's heroes are tragic. The protagonist, Charles Frank, is a young man of twenty filled with both a deep appetite for and an even deeper hatred of life. He rejects the society of his fellow Tyrolian hunters, and in a rage burns down his father's house, thus severing symbolically all ties with humanity. His bitter nihilism is explained in the soliloquy that ends act 4. Frank, like Rolla, describes himself as the child of an impious age that believes in nothing. Musset alludes to the pernicious legacy of the materialist philosophy of the previous century.

> Je renierai l'amour, la fortune et la gloire;
> Mais je crois au néant, comme je crois en moi.
> Le soleil le sait bien, qu'il n'est sous la lumière
> Qu'une immortalité, celle de la matière.

He also curses the nefarious "analyseurs" of the Enlightenment. The result of this intellectual legacy is disaster.

> L'amour n'existe plus; la vie est devastée.
> Et l'homme, resté seul, ne croit plus qu'à la mort.

This statement anticipates one of Malraux's: The death of God will bring on the death of man since the latter will be able to define himself "vertically" only in terms of the one remaining absolute: Death.

After knowing fame, wealth and sensual love, Frank soon learns to despise them, concluding like Pushkin's Boris Gudonov that

> Glory, luxury and the devilish love
> Of women seem beautiful from a distance.

He returns at the end of the play to his native village and to the childhood sweetheart, Déidamia, he had left behind. Déidamia is a symbol not only of hope for the future but of the lost purity and innocence of Frank's youth. Just moments before the nuptials are to be performed, just before the cup touches the lips, Déidamia is murdered by Frank's former mistress, Belcolore, symbol of the dangers of debauchery but, on another level, of Frank's—and modern man's—incurable doubt.

The overall thematic structure of *La Coupe*, like that of Rolla, is loosely integrated. Musset seems to switch emphasis mid-way through the poem. As Jean d'Aquitaine explains: "On croirait que le poète a voulu d'abord faire la tragédie de l'orgueil et de la puissance qu'il peut développer dans une âme, mais soudain il tourne court sur une autre donnée et fait le procès de l'inconduite, qui s'arme d'un poignard et termine le drame, malgré l'idylle du cinquième acte, par un assassinat" (*Musset le poète*, p. 65). Perhaps a determined reader could find a central unifying theme (the impossibility of happiness in a hypersensitive soul, or the impossibility of transcendence), but it is true that the author has not clearly focussed his major point.

The plot of *La Coupe* is arranged by Chance, not because of a technical flaw but for the desired philosophical implications. Frank calls himself "fils du hasard," and it is indeed Chance that throws him into the path of the beautiful and treacherous courtesan, Belcolore; it is Chance that makes him wealthy through luck at the gambling table; and it is Chance that brings him military glory rather than almost certain death in battle. The point is that since the age of Voltaire and the *philosophes* of the Enlightenment, divine providence no longer rules the universe.

> La poussière est à Dieu; — le reste est au hasard.
> (*Rolla*)

The style of *La Coupe* is declamatory, marked by long and loud monologues, rhetorical flourishes, artificial eloquence. The sentences are often periodic in structure, epic in tonality. Musset pulls out all the stops: magnification and the marvelous (if a universe ruled by Chance can be said to partake of the supernatural), repetitions, enumerations, apostrophes, extended laudations and imprecations. Let one example, a Faustian imprecation, suffice:

> Malheur aux nouveau-nés!
> Maudit soit le travail! maudite l'espérance!
> Malheur au coin de terre où germe la semence,
> Où tombe la sueur de deux bras décharnés!
> Maudits soient les liens du sang et de la vie!
> Maudite la famille et la société!
> Malheur à la maison, malheur à la cité,
> Et malédiction sur la mère patrie!

The declamatory style is appropriate to the genre: Musset is not striving for psychological realism but philosophical lyricism, something new in French poetry, and refreshing when compared to Vigny's prosaic philosophical poems.

The second contribution to the Armchair Theater is a comedy, and like many comedies it has no real hero since the idealistic, shy and self-effacing Silvio, as M. P. Van Tieghem puts it, is "nullement un caractère mais une manière d'aimer" (*Musset*, p. 44) that is, almost an abstraction. While lacking a real hero, the play is the first study of the *jeune fille* in French dramatic literature. It is a delightful comedy of fanciful plot and poetic atmosphere in the Shakespearean manner. There is no attention paid to the historical or geographical setting ("La scène est où l'on voudra"), or to authentic costumes, there is no satire on contemporary mores, no complicated imbroglio, no clever marivaudage, no bravura passages or even any *mots d'auteur* (see Van Tieghem, p. 43-44). Musset insists not on the ridiculous (although the ridiculous Irus serves as foil to Sylvio) but on the charming world of two naive adolescent girls, the twin sisters, Ninon and Ninette, who at fifteen are in love with love. With *A quoi rêvent les jeunes filles?* Musset introduces another genre new to French literature, the *comédie de fantaisie*.

The basic style of the play can be characterized as poeticized conversation. The dialogues in several scenes are contrapuntally arranged. In the following passage for instance the sisters are "on stage" together but are in two different parts of the garden; unaware of each other's presence, they are engaged not in dialogue but in a lyrical duet.

NINON
> Toi dont la voix est douce, et douce la parole,
> Chanteur mystérieux, reviendras-tu me voir?
> Ou, comme en soupirant, l'hirondelle s'envole,
> Mon bonheur fuira-t-il, n'ayant duré qu'un soir?

NINETTE
Audacieux fantôme à la forme voilée,
Les ombrages ce soir seront-ils sans danger?
Te reverrai-je encor dans cette sombre allée,
Ou disparâtras-tu comme un chamois léger?

NINON
L'eau, la terre et les vents, tout s'emplit d'harmonies.
Un jeune rossignol chante au fond de mon coeur.
J'entends sous les roseaux murmurer des génies. . .
Ai-je de nouveaux sens inconnus à ma soeur?

NINETTE
Pourquoi ne puis-je voir sans plaisir et sans peine
Les baisers du zéphyr trembler sur la fontaine,
Et l'ombre des tilleuls passer sur mes bras nus?
Ma soeur est une enfant, — et je ne le suis plus.

NINON
O fleurs des nuits d'été, magnifique nature!
O plantes! ô rameaux! l'un dans l'autre enlacés!

NINETTE
O feuilles des palmiers, reines de la verdure,
Qui versez vos amours dans les vents embrasés!

The theme of the passage is of course the awakening of the senses: Nature is seen for the first time in its sexual aspect ("baisers du zéphyr;" "rameaux enlacés;" "vents embrasés"). Seldom have Musset's charm and delicacy of touch been as effective as here.

Silvio, although more a flat than a round character, is nearly as charming in his youthful naiveté as the sisters. Like Perdican he has just recently graduated from the university; unlike Perdican he is tongue-tied when first meeting the girl he is supposed to marry. (The girls' romantic father, Laërte, an interesting character in his own right, gives Silvio his choice of fiancée and even trains his shy son-in-law in the art of seduction!) But when alone his tongue is loosened and offers experimental (for him) images ranging from clichés

Frêles comme un roseau, blondes comme les blés. . .

to preciosity

On dirait que l'aînée est l'étui de sa soeur.

And at the end of the play he indulges in a veritable flood of similes when addressing his fiancée (Ninon).

Vos yeux sont de cristal, —vos lèvres sont vermeilles
Comme ce ciel de pourpre autour de l'occident.

. . .

Votre taille flexible est comme un palmier vert;
Vos cheveux sont légers comme la cendre fine
Qui voltige au soleil autour d'un feu d'hiver.
Ils frémissent au vent comme la balsamine;
Sur votre front d'ivoire ils courent en glissant,
Comme une huile craintive au bord d'un lac d'argent.
Vos yeux sont transparents comme l'ambre fluide
Au bord du Niemen; — leur regard est limpide
Comme une goutte d'eau sur la grenade en fleurs.

. . .

Le son de votre voix est comme un bon génie
Qui porte dans ses mains un vase plein de miel.
Toute votre nature est comme une harmonie. . . .

Frank of *La Coupe* and Silvio of *A quoi rêvent* present the two basic and contrasting types of hero found in Musset's fiction and drama as well as his narrative and dramatic poetry. The first is cynical and corrupt, disillusioned with life, with his fellow man, with love, and finally with himself. The second is inexperienced, pure in body and in mind, tender, trusting, and expecting much, in fact everything, from love. It is a commonplace of Musset criticism that the two types are reflections (stylized refractions, rather) of Musset's dual personality.

*
* *

4. *Extended lyrics*

Musset's famous Night Cycle, which includes in addition to the four *Nuits* the *Lettre à Lamartine*, *L'Espoir en Dieu* and *Souvenir*, presents extended lyrics written between 1835 and 1841. Until this cycle Musset's longer poems had been narrative and dramatic, that is, impersonal. The cycle presents the poet's thoughts and feelings on poetry, love, religion, memory and life in general, but the theme that gives the cycle its profoundest unity is that of the role of suffering in the life of a poet.

The *Nuits* are usually considered elegiac *cris de coeur* (hostile critics speak of gush and mush) but in the main they explore *ideas* thanks especially to the Poet/Muse dialectic. The principal theme is not the poet's suffering per se but the relationship between suffering and poetic creativity and the relationship between suffering and love. The cycle forms an organic, if loosely knit, unit, but critics have paid scant attention to the contribution of each poem to the whole and their relationship with each other. The *Nuit de Mai* is an unresolved debate between the Poet and his Muse. The latter, who represents Musset's more energetic and positive side, insists that suffering is inspiration, the very stuff of great poetry.

> Rien ne nous rend si grands qu'une grande douleur.
> . . .
> Les plus désespérés sont les chants les plus beaux.
> Et j'en sais d'immortels qui sont de purs sanglots.

Her final argument takes the form of the famous parable of the Pelican, who lets its young feed on his heart, just as the lyric poet sacrifices his privacy and bears his soul for the spiritual and aesthetic nourishment of the public. The Poet (Musset's passive, pessimistic side—but the capital letter enlarges the debate beyond the scope of a mere personal problem), insists on the contrary that intense suffering stifles the poet's voice.

> La bouche garde le silence
> Pour écouter le coeur.
> . . .
> L'homme n'écrit rien sur le sable
> A l'heure où passe l'aquilon.

Although it is the poet who has the last word in *La Nuit de Mai* and who speaks alone in *La Nuit de Décembre*, it is the Muse's theory that is put into practice in the latter: The Poet enumerates—and in verse! — his many sorrows, thus effecting a catharsis that will eventually liberate him from sterile passivity and melancholy. At the time he wrote *La Nuit de Mai* Musset's state of mind was no doubt closer to that of the Muse than that of his persona. The Muse invites the Poet to imitate the springtime—

> Poète, prends ton luth et me donne un baiser;
> La fleur de l'églantier sent ses bourgeons éclore,
> Le printemps naît ce soir; les vents vont s'embraser.

Similarly, just before writing the *Nuit de Mai* Musset himself felt as if a new poetic phase was about to blossom forth. His brother Paul tells us that having written nothing during the Winter months of 1835 his friend Alfred Tatet asked him what would be "the fruit of his silence." Musset allegedly replied: "Aujourd'hui j'ai cloué de mes propres mains, dans la bière, ma première jeunesse, ma paresse et ma vanité. Je crois sentir enfin que ma pensée, comme une plante qui a été longtemps arosée, a puisé dans la terre des sucs pour croître au soleil. Il me semble que je vais bientôt parler et que j'ai quelque chose dans l'âme qui demande à sortir."[1] (Note in passing that Musset refers to his poetry as *pensée*, a point brought up a moment ago and one that I shall bring up again shortly and develop more fully in the next chapter.) Musset then wrote the *Nuit de Mai* in a state of exaltation, setting candles at his writing table for the Muse, and upon completing it he felt that his mental anguish had been cured.

For the cure thus effected to be a lasting one Musset needed to confront directly the anguish only hinted at in *La Nuit de Mai*. The next stage was that recommended by the Muse: *épanchement*, that is, the cathartic role of *La Nuit de Décembre*. In this second poem of the cycle most of the poet's traumatic experiences and *blocages* are made explicit: the cruel disappointments in love (three especially: his first one Mme Beaulieu, his greatest one, George Sand, and his most recent one, Mme Jaubert), the death of his father, the *hantise du double*, and the central theme, solitude.

The self-portrait presented in *La Nuit de Décembre* is that of an authentic romantic hero: We see not just the solitude, but the thirst for the absolute and the unknown ("la soif d'un monde ignoré"), the misanthropy and cynicism ("La face humaine et ses mensonges"), the eternal boredom ("le boiteux Ennui"), the death wish ("Partout où j'ai voulu mourir"). Musset's double, who haunts him at every grievous moment in his life, is described as "Un orphelin vêtu de noir"—two topoi constantly attached to the romantic *beau ténébreux*.[2]

The *Nuit de Décembre* is an elegy—the only one, incidentally, of the four *Nuits* that is a true elegy—but his grief, having come out into the open, can now be put behind him or at least faced up to. In the rest of the cycle the poet is not going to indulge in sorrow for sorrow's sake, as is often claimed or implied; he is going to try to come to grips with it. The third *Nuit* (*d'Août*), thanks to the second one, will be written in a serene mood, "son coeur guéri," according to his brother. "Ouvre tes bras," the poet joyously cries to the Muse, "je viens chanter."

In the *Nuit d'Août* the Poet is ready to deal with his greatest emotional crisis, the George Sand affair, and to work his way toward psychological liberation: He will seek love elsewhere. The poem captures the poet's frame of mind at this point in his emotional career as expressed to Sand herself (now only "a friend") in his correspondence.

> J'aurai cependant d'autres maîtresses; maintenant les arbres se couvrent de verdure et l'odeur des lilas entre ici par bouffées: tout renaît et le coeur me bondit malgré moi. Je suis encore jeune, la première femme que j'aurai sera jeune aussi. (*Correspondance*, p. 59.)

> Plus je vois de choses crouler sous mes pieds, plus je sens une force cachée qui s'élève, et se tend comme la corde d'un arc. . .
> C'est le printems. . . ce sont les fleurs et toute cette verdure qui m'appellent à la vie. (Ibid., p. 68)

> Peut-être les élégies dont mon coeur est plein vont se changer en hymne. Il me semble que la nature entière l'entonnerait avec moi. . . Je ne sais si c'est de peur ou de plaisir que je frissonne. Je vais aimer. (Ibid., p. 72)

As in these letters it is "immortal Nature" that teaches the poet that life and love must go on after tragedy.

> Puisque l'oiseau des bois voltige et chante encore
> Sur la branche où ses oeufs sont brisés dans le nid;
>
> . . .
>
> Puisque, jusqu'aux rochers, tout se charge en poussière;
> Puisque tout meurt ce soir pour revivre demain;
>
> . . .
>
> Après avoir souffert, il faut souffrir encore;
> Il faut aimer sans cesse, après avoir aimé.

The fourth and final *Nuit* (*d' Octobre*) expresses this same feeling of expectation and renewed confidence in life and in himself, but only after the poet has vented his spleen. The Muse must convince him that grief is instructive

> L'homme est un apprenti, la douleur est son maître.

and that hatred is beneath his dignity

> Tu dis vrai: la haine est impie.

He will forgive and forget the betrayals of former mistresses and think only of his new one (Aimée d'Alton).

From the polyvalent figure of the first *Nuit* the Muse becomes progressively more maternal in the *Nuit d'Août* and the *Nuit d'Octobre*, "signe évident", says Bernard Masson, "d'une remise en ordre de la psyché perturbée ("Relire les *Nuits*," p. 197). The *Nights*, collectively, tell the story of a debilitating crisis followed by an intermittent but finally successful convalescence, indeed a rebirth, the resurrection of a poet who had thought himself dead. The last verb of the last *Night* is *renaître*.

The year before he wrote *La Nuit d'Octobre* Musset began but never completed a fifth poem, *La Nuit de Juin*. Only four lines are known to us, but they are enough to indicate clearly the central theme and tone:

> Muse, quand le blé pousse, il faut être joyeux.
> Regarde ces coteaux et leur blonde parure.
> Quelle douce clarté dans l'immense nature!
> Tout ce qui vit ce soir doit se sentir heureux.

One has only to compare the bright joyous imagery of these lines with the darker hues of the first two *Nuits* to see how far Musset has evolved during the course of the cycle.

> Comme il fait noir dans la vallée!
> (*Nuit de Mai*)

> Un malheureux vêtu de noir
> Qui me ressemblait comme un frère.
> (*Nuit de Décembre*)

The basic style of the night cycle can be called oratorical lyricism. Repetitions, apostrophes, long enumerations and anaphoras, rhetorical questions and exclamations abound. The poet is not even averse to using what he has often decried: the ornamental periphrasis. The month of June for instance, is presented thus:

> Depuis que le soleil, dans l'horizon immense,
> A franchi le Cancer sur son axe enflammé. . .

and the moon becomes "l'astre cher au voyageur." The oratory, which at times borders on the declamatory, does not derive from any lack of spontaneity and sincerity. On the contrary, declamation and intense emotion, as the Muse knows well, often go hand in hand.

> Leurs déclamations sont comme des épées.
> Elles tracent dans l'air un cercle éblouissant,
> Mais il y pend toujours quelques gouttes de sang.
> (*Nuit de Mai*)

Spontaneous, not studied, eloquence is indeed one of the marks of Musset's style.

There are two reasons why the *Nuits* do not degenerate into maudlin sentimentality. The first is the dramatic form they are given. The dark brooding of the Dionysian poet is countered, writes Russell King, by the restraint of the Apollonian Muse; or, as Bernard Masson puts it, the darker side of the poet's Jungian *Selbst* is confronted by his *Anima*. The long, well constructed and harmonious sentences of the Muse give a sense of controlled emotion, of clarity and logic. She speaks in stately alexandrines while the tense, impulsive Poet often speaks in shorter lines and shorter sentences punctuated by anguished questions and exclamations and uneven or staccato rhythms created by an enjambement, a displaced caesura, a seven-syllable line ("Honte à toi qui la première") or a six-syllable line followed by an octosyllable. Upon rereading the *Nuits* Alphonse Bouvet was struck by "leur apparent décousu et leurs contradictions" ("Musset, l'amour. . ." p. 207). However the Muse/Poet debate, which inhibits perfect unity of theme and tone, and the sudden changes of mood within the Poet himself are but other aspects of the dramatic nature of these highly original lyrics.

The second reason is the surprising emphasis on general ideas rather than on the unique situation of Alfred de Musset. When the Poet alludes to his sorrow in *La Nuit de Mai*

> Mais j'ai souffert un dur martyre

the specific nature of the *martyre* is not explained. And in the other *Nuits* the culpable women remain anonymous and tend to be presented on an abstract level: *la femme* rather than *cette femme*. The Poet too is depersonalized by the capital P and by the abstract tenor of most of his argument.

> L'homme n'écrit rien sur le sable
> A l'heure où passe l'aquilon.

La bouche garde le silence
Pour écouter *le* coeur.

Leurs déclamations sont comme des épées

Rien ne *nous* rend si grands qu'*une* grande douleur.

Il faut aimer sans cesse. . .

Muse, quand le blé pousse, *il faut* être joyeux.

This generalized, intellectualized and depersonalized lyric stance escaped the notice of nineteenth-century critics. To René Doumic goes the honor of having first discovered or at least elaborated on the *flou voulu* of the *Nuits*. Writing in 1897 he establishes an important fact:

> Le plus frappant, dans les *Nuits*, c'est de voir comment le poète y dépouille son émotion de tous les éléments particuliers, de tous les détails qui l'auraient faite étroite et précise. . . Les personnes, les noms, le décor extérieur, le lieu, la date, autant de détails que nous sommes libres d'imaginer à notre gré. . . Telle est pour la poésie lyrique elle-même, la condition de vie et de la durée: il faut qu'elle dépasse les émotions d'un homme et l'expression des sentiments d'un jour, pour arriver jusqu'à ce fond immuable et commun où, par delà les individus et les temps, toutes les souffrances humaines se reconnaissent et se répondent.
> (Quoted by P. Gastinel, *Romantisme de Musset*, p. 493)

Thus Doumic sees Musset striving for universality. Joachim Merlant thinks rather that it is a sense of delicacy that impels poets like Musset to speak in general rather than specific terms: "l'expression verbale jette toujours une lumière trop nette, trop crue sur les sentiments. Aussi les poètes de la vie intérieure, Musset, Vigny, Lamartine, Verlaine, se sont-ils de plus en plus préoccupés de trouver une forme indécise, flottante, qui parle aux seuls initiés; c'est à la fois un scrupule de délicatesse morale et de probité artistique. A vouloir dire complètement certaines choses on les trahit"(*Musset: morceaux choisis*, p. 101). Margaret Rees (*Musset*, p. viii) is impressed with how much "food for thought" there is to be found in Musset's work and submits (p. 65) that the important role of ideas in the *Poésies nouvelles* has been soft-pedaled by the critics. Philippe Van Tieghem (*Musset:, p. 21*) is convinced that the most striking characteristic of the *Nuits* is the primacy of the intellectual, and Patricia Siegel ("Structure et thématique," chapter 2) calls them the apogee of Musset's thought.

The style of the other three poems in the cycle is similar to that of the four *Nuits*. The *Lettre à M. de Lamartine* (1836) is addressed, with considerable rhetorical flourish, to the Christian poet and especially the poet of sorrow with whom Musset now identifies thanks to his new feeling that great pain is providential (*Nuit d'Octobre*). As with nearly all the poems in the cycle the movement is from autobiographical allusions (here the second and final *rupture* with Mme Jaubert, mingled as usual with his first disappointment in love) to more general considerations, from the particular to the universal. Musset affirms his belief in a vaguely perceived God and in the immortality of the soul, which will eventually triumph over its transient grief and preserve for eternity the memory of true love. This final theme is expressed in oratory that has been both praised for its "incomparable" forcefulness and damned for its grandiloquence.

> Tu te sens le coeur pris d'un caprice de femme,
> Et tu dis qu'il se brise à force de souffrir.
> Tu demandes à Dieu de soulager ton âme:
> Ton âme est immortelle, et ton coeur va guérir.
>
> Le regret d'un instant te trouble et te dévore;
> Tu dis que le passé te voile l'avenir.
> Ne te plains pas d'hier; laisse venir l'aurore:
> Ton âme est immortelle, et le temps va s'enfuir.
>
> Ton corps est abattu du mal de ta pensée;
> Tu sens ton front peser et tes genoux fléchir.
> Tombe, agenouille-toi, créature insensée:
> Ton âme est immortelle, et la mort va venir.
>
> Tes os dans le cercueil vont tomber en poussière;
> Ta mémoire, ton nom, ta gloire vont périr,
> Mais non pas ton amour, si ton amour t'est chère:
> Ton âme est immortelle, et va s'en souvenir.

L'Espoir en Dieu, despite the title and apparent theme, expresses an anguish more than a faith. The deliberative monologue and the fluctuating feelings that develop as the poem progresses are dramatic, not dogmatic. The poem registers the musings of a doubter who "wants" to believe. There are Pascalian echoes: the anguish before the infinite—

> Malgré moi l'infini me tourmente. .
> Je n'y saurais songer sans crainte et sans espoir.

and a theological wager of sorts—

> Pour que Dieu nous réponde, adressons-nous à lui.
>
> . . .
>
> Si le ciel est désert, nous n'offensons personne:
> Si quelqu'un nous entend, qu'il nous prenne en pitié!

The final section, however, presents almost accusatory questions

> Pourquoi fais-tu douter de toi?
> Quel triste plaisir peux-tu prendre
> A tenter notre bonne foi?
>
> Pourquoi donc, ô Maître suprême,
> As-tu créé le mal si grand?

and a challenge

> Soulève les voiles du monde
> Et montre-toi, Dieu juste et bon!

Souvenir offers the cycle's final statement on the problem of ephemeral love. It is a development of the optimism expressed in the *Lettre à Lamartine*. Life's rare privileged moments do endure: in the memory, in poetry, and in the soul's immortal consciousness. The poem belongs to a genre that Meyer Abrams has called the greater Romantic lyric. We will examine the genre and look closely at the style of *Souvenir* in chapter seven.

Two other extended lyrics of note are *A la Malibran* (1838) and *Souvenir des Alpes* (1852). The first holds little interest for the reader of the late twentieth century for two reasons: the subject and the style. Musset himself explains in the elegy that while great painters and poets live eternally through the works that survive them, the art of a great singer is lost to posterity. The magnificent voice of La Malibran could not be recorded then as now, and so her fame gradually died out with the passing generations. Another thematic problem is the idealization of an undoubtedly dedicated artist who died prematurely; she died, in fact, not so much the victim of her dedication to her art and her public, and not the victim of her fiery genius, as the poem claims, but from a fall off a horse. And the 25 rhetorical questions (more than 46% of the poem's sentences and more the 64% of the sentences in the middle section—stanzas 8 to 24—) become tiresome to the modern reader. *Souvenir des Alpes*, like the more famous *Souvenir*, is another good example of the greater Romantic lyric and will be discussed from this generic perspective in an appendix.

The originality of Musset's lyricism should be stressed. Despite the poetics of the *Nuit de Mai* (which will be put in its proper perspective in the next chapter), Musset's extended lyrics are *not* simple *cris de coeur,* mere developments of an exclamation. They move consistently from the personal to the general and belong as much to the poetry of ideas as to traditional lyricism. One critic, Yves Le Hir, has noticed the high frequency of maxims and aphorisms in Musset's love lyrics. Even in the many exclamatory and interrogative sentences it is usually an *idea,* not a complaint, that is being developed lyrically.

*

* *

5. Satirical Poetry

Further proof that Musset's opus contains a poetry of ideas is the fact that a substantial portion of it is devoted to another genre, satirical poetry. His measuring stick for objects of satire is the usual one: common sense ("le bon sens, he says, "fait parler le génie.")

> . . . l'éternel bon sens, lequel est né français.
> ("Sur la paresse")

The main target of his satirical barbs is the new romantic school, or, rather, the diffuse romantic movement, which was trying to consolidate itself into a school. His first complaint against romanticism is that much of it offends, again, common sense.

> Ma lanterne est vraiment magique:
> Pour un sous vous verrez cela.
> Un intrigant qui fuit le monde;
> Une femme qui se vieillit;
> Un jeune avocat sans faconde;
> Un grand médecin qui guérit.
>   . . .
> Un mélodrame sans horreurs;
> Le bon sens chez un romantique.
> ("La Lanterne magique")

In the utopian society of which the naive Dupont dreams ("Dupont et Durand") there will be a reconciliation of opposites and of enemies: the Russian with the Turk, the Englishman with France, religious faith with indifference, and "the modern (i.e., romantic) drama with common sense." He attacked stereotyped romantic themes such as that automatic ecstasy experienced by young romantic poets when observing Nature's beauties, and the elegiac lyrics mass-produced by the disciples of Lamartine.

> Mais je hais les pleurards, les rêveurs à nacelle,
> Les amants de la nuit, des lacs, des cascatelles,
> Cette engeance sans nom, qui ne peut faire un pas
> Sans s'inonder de vers, de pleurs, et d'agendas.
> ("Dédicace" to La Coupe et les Lèvres)

He attacked romanticism's insistence on rich rhyme, its penchant for prefaces, its borrowings from foreign literatures, its .utopian social schemes, its bad French, the complicated and implausible plots of its drama, its stereotyped hero (le beau ténébreux), its superficial local color and its abuse of adjectives of color.

Another frequent topic of satire is journalism, especially journalistic criticism.

> O critique du jour, chère mouche bovine,
> Que te voilà pédante au troisième degré!
> Quel plaisir ce doit être, à ce que j'imagine
> D'aiguiser sur un livre un museau de fouine!
>
> Et de ronger à l'ombre un squelette ignoré!
> J'aime à te voir surtout, en style de cuisine,
> Te comparer sans honte au poète inspiré
> Et gonfler ta grenouille aux pieds du boeuf sacré!
>
> Oh! que je t'aime ainsi, dépeçant tout d'abord
> Quiconque autour de toi donne signe de vie,
> Et puis, d'un laurier-rose, amer comme l'envie,
> Couronnant un chacal sur le ventre d'un mort!
> ("Aux critiques de *Chatterton*")

Other targets were his century

> Ce qu'on fait aujourd'hui, on le dit, et la cause
> En est bien naturelle: on fait si peu de chose.
> ("Une bonne fortune")

the French Academy (before Musset himself was inducted of course), the sacrosanct park at Versailles ("Sur trois marches de marbre rose"), the British, Saint-Simon and Fourier. In "L'Anglaise en diligence" he pokes fun at the English for their phlegmatic reserve and their insensitivity to grammatical gender when speaking French.

> Nous étions douze ou treize
> Les uns sur les autres pressés,
>   Entassés,
>   . . .
> A mon droite une squelette
>   A mon gauche une athlète,
> Les os du premier il me perçait;
> Les poids du second il m'écrasait.
>   . . .
> La poussière, il me suffoquait,
> Puis un méchant enfant criait,
> Et son nourrice il le battait,
>   . . .
> Pour moi, ce qui me touche,
> C'est que jusqu'au Pérou l'Anglais peut voyager
>   Sans qu'il ouvre son bouche
> —Autre que pour boire ou pour manger.

In "Sur la paresse" he lists all the major ills of his country and his century: modern journalism is placed at the top of the list; then comes hypocrisy, mediocrity, lack of faith, love of money and sensual pleasure, utopian socialism and finally political fanaticism capable of assassination. German chauvinism and jingoism are vigorously satirized in *Le Rhin allemand*, but this is a spur-of-the-moment repartee to a provocation, not a subject of perpetual concern.

Rather than belaboring the ideas, it would be more profitable and pertinent to our purpose to examine briefly Musset's satirical style. The first point must be that Musset's natural verve makes of him the best satirist among the major romantics and one of the best of his century. In the rollicking "Revue romantique" he pokes fun at friends and enemies alike in terse, droll vignettes. Here is Sainte-Beuve

> Heureux qui n'a pas vu le pensif Sainte-Beuve,
> Pour son coeur dévoyé cherchant une âme soeur,
> Durant les soirs d'été répandre, comme un fleuve,
> Ses mystiques sermons et sa molle sueur.

and Balzac

> Heureux qui n'a pas vu Balzac le drôlatique
> Lire, en bavant partout, *la Femme de trente ans.*
> Et, tout ébouriffé de sa verve lubrique,
> De romans inconnus foirant une fabrique,
> Cracher, au trait final, ses trois dernières dents!

and Vigny

> Heureux qui n'a pas vu, le soir, dans la coulisse,
> Errer sur les débris d'un proverbe tombé
> Le pâle de Vigny, vieux cygne en pain d'épice,
> Promenant son oeil sombre et ses bons mots d'abbé!

His satirical descriptions reveal his talent for depicting the grotesque; this *valseuse* for example.

> Quand Madame W(aldor) à P(aul) F(oucher) s'accroche,
>   Montrant le tartre de ses dents,
> Et dans la valse en feu, comme l'huître à la roche,
>   S'incruste à ses muscles ardents;
>
>   . . .
>
> Quand la molle sueur qui de son sein ruisselle
>   Comme l'huile d'un vieux quinquet,
> Sur ses pieds avachis tombant de son aisselle
>   Fait des desseins sur le parquet;
>   ("A une Muse")

The description is delightful in itself, but the poem's subtitle provides
an added dimension to the satire: This unprepossessing lady is an official
Muse of the romantic Cénacle! The physical description of Durand and
Dupont, two romantic *ratés*, is symbolic of their intellectual mediocrity.

DURAND

Que vois-je donc là bas? Quel est ce pauvre diable
Qui dans ses doigts transis souffle avec désespoir,
Et rôde en grelottant sous un mince habit noir?

. . .

DUPONT

Je ne me trompe pas. Ce morne et plat visage,
Cet oeil sombre et penaud, ce front préoccupé,
Sur ces longs cheveux gras ce grand chapeau râpé
C'est mon ami Durand, mon ancien camarade.

His portrait of the envious writer, in the same poem, is worthy of La
Bruyère.

Ah! Dupont, qu'il est doux de tout déprécier!
Pour un esprit mort-né, convaincu d'impuissance,
Qu'il est doux d'être un sot et d'en tirer vengeance!
A quelque vrai succès lorsqu'on vient d'assister,
Qu'il est doux de rentrer et de se débotter,
Et de dépecer l'homme, et de salir sa gloire,
Et de pouvoir sur lui vider une écritoire,
Et d'avoir quelque part un journal inconnu
Où l'on puisse à plaisir nier ce qu'on a vu!
Le mensonge anonyme est le bonheur suprême.

Adopting a trick of Byron's, Musset will frequently insert foreign words
for satirical as well as purely comic effect. Anglicisms are used in *Mardoche*
and *Les Marrons* to suggest that the anglophilia of the romantic period
has degenerated into anglomania; in the following line for instance the
deliberate clumsiness of the English phrase and the eleven-syllable line
(*vers boiteux*) underscore the inappropriateness of aping English manners
and speech.

And how do you do, mon bon père, aujourd'hui?

Other favorite devices are the sarcastic epithet and simile. Journalistic
critics are called "chercheurs de vermine," "moucherons" "mouches
bovines," "fouines;" the gullible public is called "peuple gobe-mouche;"
the utopian socialists are called "chercheurs d'avenir," their doctrines
summed up as "humanitairerie" (Musset's work is not rich in neologisms);

Durand's romantic skull is "ossianique." At the beginning of *Namouna*
his hero is naked; naked as a church wall, naked as a silver platter, but
also naked as the speech of an Academician. The classical alexandrine,
viciously violated by the romantics, has its own problem: monotony.

> L'âme et le corps, hélas! ils iront deux à deux,
> Tant que le monde ira, —pas à pas, —côte à côte,
> Comme s'en vont les vers classiques et les boeufs.
> (*Namouna*)

Musset's satirical strategies are impressively varied. He uses the
hyperbolic definition—

> D'abord, le grand fléau qui nous rend tous malades,
> Le seigneur Journalisme et ses pantalonnades;
> Ce droit quotidien qu'un sot a de berner
> Trois ou quatre milliers de sots, à déjeuner. . .
> ("Sur la paresse")

the windy generalization—

> Pour moi, ce qui me touche,
> C'est que jusqu'au Pérou l'Anglais peut voyager
> Sans qu'il ouvre la bouche
> —Autre que pour boire ou pour manger.
> ("L'Anglaise en diligence")

the *reductio ad absurdum*

> L'univers, mon ami, sera bouleversé,
> On ne verra plus rien qui ressemble au passé!
> Les riches seront gueux et les nobles infâmes;
> Nos maux seront des biens, les hommes seront femmes. . . .
> Du reste, on ne verra, mon cher, dans les campagnes,
> Ni forêts, ni clochers, ni vallons, ni montagnes:
> Chansons que tout cela! Nous les supprimerons,
> Nous les démolirons, comblerons, brûlerons.
> ("Dupont et Durand")

the facetious, deflationary *rime équivoquée*—

> Debout ruisselant comme un fleuve,
> Sainte-Beuve;
> . . .
> Baour, sourd de ses vers qu'il beugle
> En aveugle,
> Allait chantant d'un ton sciant
> Ossian.

Dans tes culottes sans brettelles,
    Lacretelle,
Dis-moi, prolixe historien,
    N'est-il rien?
D'un homme tu n'es pas le tiers,
    Petit Thiers.
De peur de devenir enceinte,
    Quand ta sainte,
Se gare au lit . . . de son époux . . .
    Non, des poux.
    . . .
Chaque jour leur chantant matines
    Lamartine
Rappelle à ses souscripteurs
    Ses malheurs.
("Satire contre l'Académie")

— the derisive subtitle

COMPLAINTE
Historique et véritable
Sur le Fameux Duel Qui a eu Lieu
Entre Plusieurs
Hommes de Plume
Très inconnus dans Paris, à l'occasion
D'un livre
Dont il a été beaucoup parlé
De Différentes Manières
Ainsi qu'il est relaté dans la
Présente Complainte.

Of course the ultimate satirical insult would be to call one's target unworthy even of satire. This device too is used.

Non, mon cher, Dieu merci! pour trois mots de critique
Je ne me suis pas fait poète satirique;
    . . .
Mais censurer les sots, que le ciel m'en préserve!
Quand je m'en sentirais la chaleur et la verve,
Dans ce triste combat dussé-je être vainqueur,
Le dégoût que j'en ai m'en ôterait le coeur.
    ("A Alfred Tatet")

Wondering what the great satirist of the seventeenth century, Mathurin Régnier, would have said of the nineteenth, Musset concludes:

Il eût trouvé ce siècle indigne de satire,
Trop vain pour en pleurer, trop triste pour en rire.
    ("Sur la paresse")

One of Musset's most impressive performances as a satirist is "Sur une morte." His theme is the cold, unfeeling young beauty who has refused his advances. It is handled deftly with dispassionate delicacy. The opening attack is gentle and the increasing harshness so gradual as to be almost imperceptible. But with an enumeration of if-clauses, the poet cleverly derides the young woman not so much by the logic of his arguments as by the weight of his examples.

> Elle était belle, si la Nuit
> Qui dort dans la sombre chapelle
> Où Michel-Ange a fait son lit,
> Immobile, peut être belle.
>
> Elle était bonne, s'il suffit
> Qu'en passant la main s'ouvre et donne,
> Sans que Dieu n'ait rien vu, rien dit,
> Si l'or sans pitié fait l'aumone.
>
> Elle aurait pleuré, si sa main
> Sur son coeur froidement posée,
> Eût jamais, dans l'argile humain,
> Senti la céleste rosée.
>
> Elle aurait aimé, si l'orgueil,
> Pareil à la lampe inutile
> Qu' on allume près d'un cercueil,
> N'eût veillé sur son coeur stérile.
>
> Elle est morte, n'a point vécu.
> Elle faisait semblant de vivre.
> De ses mains est tombé le livre
> Dans lequel elle n'a rien lu.

*

* *

6. *Some Generalities*

While Musset's thematic range is somewhat limited— Henry James
speaks of "his contented smallness of horizon"— the stylistic range of
his poetry is impressively wide. It extends, as we have seen, from the
simplest of styles, at times mere prose plus meter and rhyme, to rhetorical
eloquence and declamatory grandiloquence. It is what one might call
his middle register that critics have most appreciated, those passages and
entire poems marked by grace or wit and especially by a certain lightness
of touch that elicit epithets of praise such as *ailé, aérien*.

Other critics, especially Margaret Rees and M. Sutcliffe, have singled
out Musset's animating imagery for praise.

> Sur l'ivoire
> Ses doigts légers allaient sautant
> Et chantant. . .
> ("Réponse a M. Charles Nodier")

With a transferred epithet fingers will become "inquiets" ("Une bonne
fortune"), a lorgnon "indiscret" (*Mardoche*), hands "harmonieuses" ("A
Ninon") a blouse "amoureux" ("A mon frère revenant d'Italie.") With
a syllepsis the human will be joined to the inanimate.

> Et laissez vos regards avec le vin couler.
> (*Les Marrons*)
> . . . j'ai soufflé de colère
> Ma bougie et ma verve, et je me suis couché.
> (*Namouna*)

And with a catachresis a finger will "sing," an eye will "babble."

Animism is frequently achieved through the personification of
abstractions.

> Nous n'avons fait que rire, et causé un moment,
> Quand sa vivacité coudoya ma paresse.
> ("A M. Régnier, après la mort da sa fille")

Occasionally Musset indulges in pompous, solemn allegory.

> L'Espérance et la Mort se sont donné la main,
> Et traversant ainsi la terre désolée,
> L'une marche à pas lents, toujours calme et voilée;
> Sur ses genoux tremblants l'autre tombe en chemin,
> Et se traîne en pleurant meurtrie et mutilée.
> ("Le treize juillet")

More often a personified abstraction is handled with the poet's usual lightness of touch.

> Lorsque la coquette Espérance
> Nous pousse le coude en passant,
> Puis à tire d'aile s'élance,
> Et se retourne en souriant. . .
>
> ("Chanson")

In other pieces Poverty stretches out her thin hand to Hospitality ("Invocation"), Debauchery plants a nail in the breast of the debauched (*La Coupe*), Madness shake's its fool's bells ("Idylle"); while Virginity hides timorously in large cities, Corruption will offer a brazen kiss to Prostitution (*Rolla*).

The wide variety of genres in Musset's poetic opus should surprise those readers who have identified him exclusively with the extended lyric. Even more interesting is the fact that for Musset, just as for many romantic poets, distinctions of genre tend to break down, or more accurately, the old relations between genre and style become ambiguous, the poetic text becomes polyphonic. John P. Houston is one of the few critics to stress this important feature of Musset's poetry. We have already seen most of the specific devices that Houston enumerates: the insouciance and improvisations of the Byronic verse tale; the mixture of classical alexandrines with the romantic trimeter; the *césure mobile* and radical enjambement (it was Musset who introduced the alexandrine cut 7/5); the mixture of ornamental epithets, neoclassical periphrases and the "noble" synonym with colloquial words and willfully prosaic lines; the use of *vers mêlés* and *rimes mêlées* (e.g., the *sixain* with arbitrarily disposed rhymes).

Houston has correctly asserted that this mixture of styles is the single most characteristic trait of Musset's poetry and has given some cogent analyses to prove the point. Here, for example, is what he says of *Souvenir*.

> [*Souvenir*] is a meandering, allusive poem full of startling shifts in style and topic. . . and is constructed as a fragmentary dialogue, the poet addressing as many as nine different persons or things in the course of it. . . Conventional solemnity and descriptions. . . are followed by passages of considerable novelty. . . At times he achieves the crabbed but witty tone of the metaphysicals. . . The difference we immediately note between "La Tristesse d'Olympio" and "Souvenir" is that Hugo's poem is smooth and elegant in its imagery, orotund

in tone, and based on impersonal commonplaces, whereas
Musset likes colloquialisms, ironic allusion, brusque changes
of mood, and rhetorical figures which range from the banal
to the freakish.
(*The Demonic Imagination*, pp. 37-39)

The most obvious manifestation of this mingling of styles is the
juxtaposition of the serious and the comic. (Musset's theater carried out
one part at least of Hugo's program: the *mélange des genres*.) Few critics
have discussed Musset as a humorous poet, although, as Anne Greet has
noted, he is "perhaps the first French poet since the Renaissance to make
of the humorous poem a vehicle for impulses essentially lyrical, always
expecting La Fontaine: ("Humor," p. 175). Greet lists some of Musset's
comic devices in his early poetry: the adaptation of noises—of sneezes,
hums, coughs and exclamations— to a meter habitually associated with
the expression of exalted emotion; the use of enjambement, not for pathos
but for deflation, to emphasize dull words and awkward phrasing, to
render a statement ambiguous or a dramatic situation trivial; the
fragmentation of the line; the introduction into the alexandrine of slangy
expressions, prose rhythms, inelegant imagery and homely detail. Another
comic device is to use foreign words as rhyme-words (e.g., *lazzaroni/
macaroni*).

The structure of Musset's longer poems is, to use Edward Stankiewicz'
typology, centrifugal rather than centripetal. The effect of the whole is
that of an aggregate of loose heterogeneous patterns. Rather than a tightly
integrated structure there is a discontinuous or granular structure. As
is obvious in *La Coupe* and *Rolla* and less obvious in *Souvenir*, there
is a tension between the whole and the parts, between unity and diversity,
the whole tending to be subservient to the parts. The connections between
the parts are often open and ill defined. The discreteness of the line and
the stanza breaks down in the early verse (*Mardoche, Les Marrons*) through
the use of deliberately weak rhyme, of function-words used as rhyme-
words, and of exaggerated enjambement.

The emphasis, throughout the entire opus, tends to be on the detail
for its own sake: (1) the unusual and extended metaphor and simile [—
the very fact that such images are rare in Musset's work gives special
emphasis to them, like a cadenza in a concerto or a bravura passage
in an opera, as *local effects*—]; (2) the sewing together of fragments; (3)
the frequent digressions; (4) the lack of strong terminal closure in works
like *Les Marrons* and *Portia*; (5) the oxymoron; (6) paranomasia, the
pun and the frequent wordplay with signs pertaining simultaneously

to different codes or semantic fields; (7) the conceit and the arresting single line; (8) sounds emphasized for their own sake, sometimes for comic effect, just as often for euphonic effect, as will be shown in chapter 8; (9) the foregrounding, in his first manner, of colors, ornaments, exotic names, foreign words, neologisms and archaisms and, throughout the opus, rhetorical figures, artifices, the use of the learned allusion and other kinds of extratextual reference; (10) the deconstruction of the hero in pieces like *Mardoche, Namouna* and the "Secrètes pensées de Rafaël;" (11) the affectation of nonchalance and the raising of negligence to artifice; (12) the generic ambivalence of pieces like "Une soirée perdue" where he moves from indignation to a light-hearted digression and mingles satire with elegy, or "Après une lecture" where he moves from pleasantry to genuine emotion to irony, or "Sur la paresse" where he moves quickly from disdain to anger to impassioned lyricism; (13) the mixing of styles, meters, rhyme schemes, and lexical registers; (14) the frequent renunciation of a unified point of view or tonality.

Sainte-Beuve had noticed the centrifugal structure of Musset's work as early as 1833: "M. de Musset ne paraît pas s'être inquiété jusqu'ici d'établir en son talent une force concentrique et régnante: il embrasse beaucoup, il s'élance très-haut en tous sens, mais il brise, il bouleverse à plaisir; il se plaît à aller, puis soudain à rebrousser; il accouple exprès les contraires" (*Revue des Deux Mondes*, 15 janv., 1833, p. 182)

The most important philosophical implication of this centrifugal style is the rejection of the optimistic world view of the eighteenth century, the chief heuristic model for which was the well-oiled, smoothly running machine. Musset's world—as we will see in chapter four— is a hectic and disordered one: things, people and events tend to run in opposite, multiple or contradictory directions, at cross purposes, to run away from the center, from unity and harmony, and from what they need most: love. The most optimistic model that Musset will offer for his world view is an ambivalent one: an erratic, bumpy treadmill (love) on which his protagonists and personae are constantly jumping on, falling off, and jumping on again:

Il faut aimer sans cesse, après avoir aimé.

Which means:

Après avoir souffert, il faut souffrir encore.

chapter three
MUSSET'S POETICS

Musset never wrote an official *ars poetica*. In fact he was rather violently opposed to poetics on principle, the principle being his mistrust of all rigid philosophical systems, aesthetic or other. He particularly despised the facile theories of journalistic critics.

> Les journaux sont insipides, — ces critiques sont si plats.
> Faites des systèmes, mes amis, établissez des règles, vous ne
> travaillez que sur les froids monuments du passé. Qu'un homme
> de génie se présente, et il renversera votre échafaudage et se
> rira de vos poétiques.
> *(Correspondance*, p. 11)

> J'ai rencontré Eugène Delacroix, un soir, en rentrant du
> spectacle; nous avons causé peinture, en pleine rue, de sa porte
> à la mienne et de ma porte à la sienne, jusqu'à deux heures
> du matin. . . Avec le bon Antony Deschamps, sur le boulevard,
> j'ai discuté de huit heures du soir à onze heures. Quand je sors
> de chez Nodier ou de chez Achille [Dévéria], je discute tout le
> long des rues avec l'un ou l'autre. En sommes-nous plus avancés?
> En fera-t-on un vers meilleur dans un poème, un trait meilleur
> dans un tableau? Chacun de nous a dans le ventre un certain
> son qu'il peut rendre, comme un violon ou une clarinette. Tous
> les raisonnements du monde ne pourraient faire sortir du gosier
> d'un merle la chanson du sansonnet.
> (Ibid., p. 27)

But he did write often, if unsystematically, of his conception of poetry and of the role of the poet. When his dispersed ideas are collected in one place, as here, one can appreciate their logical coherence.

*
* *

1. *The Role of Emotion and Self-expression*

In the Preface to the *Contes* Musset reminds his readers that "Clarissa Harlowe portait des paniers," an allusion to the fact that fashions change with changing times, that a work of art should not be judged by the immutable laws of absolute beauty but in the spirit of relativism. The relativity of taste, which can be taken as the first principle of Musset's poetics, was of course one of the cornerstones of French romanticism,

54

and Musset remained a romantic in this respect despite his admiration for the great classical writers of the *grand siècle*.

> Est-ce une loi pour tous qu'un siècle dans l'histoire?
>   · · ·
> Vivons-nous sous Louis quatorzième du nom?
>   ("La loi sur la presse")

> Quel que soit notre respect pour les écrivains du grand siècle, nous sommes dans d'autres conditions qu'eux; nous devons donc faire autre chose que ce qu'ils ont fait.
>   (*Oeuvres complètes*, p. 902)

But to Musset relativism also meant that romanticism should not try to establish itself as an absolute. In an age of unbelief, with no central and abiding faith, all schools should be closed, the writer should work independently: "Dans un siècle où il n'y a que l'homme, qu'on ferme les écoles" (ibid., p. 854). The main thrust of the Preface to the *Contes* is that the quarrel between romanticism and classicism has proved nothing.

By temperament Musset was the most romantic of the romantics, but his attitude toward romanticism as a movement or school, that is, as it became institutionalized, was sarcastic to the extreme. He deflated its clichés, harpooned its idealisms (there were many), ridiculed its worship of Nature, and satirized its many attempts to define itself. He was the "spoiled brat of romanticism," at once its chief exemplar and its chief detractor.

The poet must work independently not only of literary schools but of political parties. Although briefly and lukewarmly sympathetic to the Revolution of 1830, even participating in it if we are to believe his mother, he was at the same time distressed by the fact that the revolution had instantly turned artists into activists, poetry into propaganda. In "Les Voeux stériles" he catches the new politicized mood of France with bitter irony.

> Qu'est la pensée, hélas, quand l'action commence?
>   · · ·
>   Et toi, misérable poète,
> Qui que tu sois, enfant, homme, si ton coeur bat,
> Agis, jette la lyre; au combat, au combat!

The tone here is ambivalent, suggesting a dilemma, but the underlying mood is one of discouragement: he admits the priority of action to art in times of crisis, but bewails the demise of poetry during such times. In "Sur la paresse" he will express his thought in a different form of irony: the true poet must work in aristocratic leisure, in a spirit of "laziness," free from the practical concerns of politics or profession. A year after the July Revolution he writes in one of his "Revues fantastiques:" "Si la littérature veut exister, il faut qu'elle rompe en visière à la politique. Autrement, toutes deux se ressembleront, et la réalité vaudra toujours mieux que l'apparence" (*Oeuvres complètes*, p. 821). The same year he wrote in *Le Temps*: "Un poète peut parler de lui, de ses amis, des vins qu'il boit, de la maîtresse qu'il a ou voudrait avoir, du temps qu'il fait, des morts et des vivants, des sages et des fous, mais il ne doit pas faire de politique" (*Oeuvres complètes en prose*, p. 777). The sarcasm directed at the ideas of Saint-Simon and Fourier in the *Lettres de Depuis et Cotonet* is echoed in his poetry, notably in *Dupont et Durand*. The poet's mission is to promote beauty, not causes. This is the second principle of his poetics, linking him to the art for art's sake movement, which was developing precisely in the 1830's as a reaction to the *littérature engagée* of late romanticism. Musset will turn the classical axiom, "Rien n'est beau que le vrai," completely around: "Rien n'est vrai que le beau" ("Après une lecture").

However, this does not mean that the poet must remain aloof from his times; on the contrary, he must become the interpreter of the modern soul.

> Notre siècle a ses moeurs, partant, sa vérité;
> Celui qui l'ose dire est toujours écouteé
> ("Une soirée perdue")

Writing in 1833 ("Un mot sur l'art moderne") he distinguishes between two types of literature: the "classical," which studies *l'homme éternel*— a creature who has never existed, he says— and "modern," which portrays the unique temper of the times. His so-called "romantic" colleagues are placed among the classicists since beneath the medieval trappings or the Spanish local color one finds only the same vague universal man, whereas writers like Juvenal, Shakespeare and Byron have painted the *Zeitgeist* of their period. Musset claims that it is the "moderns" who have written the truest literature. This line of reasoning is close to that of Stendhal, who ten years earlier (*Racine et Shakespeare*) was defining romanticism in terms of modernism. The difference is that Musset refuses to define modernism in terms of romanticism. But one can justifiably label this "call for" modernism—the third principle of Musset's poetics— as a basic precept of an essentially romantic aesthetics.

If the poet is to paint the spirit of his times, his chief model must be himself.

> Il n'existe qu'un être
> Que je puisse en entier et constamment connaître,
> Sur qui mon jugement puisse au moins faire foi,
> Un seul!. . . Je le méprise.—Et cet être, c'est moi.
> ("Les Voeux stériles")

He must paint himself not in what he shares with all men of all times but in his uniqueness. Poetry, then, is conceived as self-expression; this is the fourth principle of his poetics and is an extension of, not a contradiction to, the third. It is the poet's duty to offer the public the most intimate, deep and heartfelt of his passions. The famous parable of the Pelican (*Nuit de Mai*) speaks to this point.

For Musset love, its ecstasies and its pains, is man's greatest emotion and therefore poetry's most important theme. "La poésie, chez moi, est soeur de l'amour. L'un fait naître l'autre et ils viennent toujours ensemble" (*Correspondance*, p. 16).

> Je vous dirai quelqu'un qui sait que je vous aime:
> C'est ma Muse, Ninon; nous avons nos secrets.
> Ma Muse vous ressemble, ou plutôt, c'est vous-même;
> Pour que je l'aime encor elle vient sous vos traits.
> ("A Ninon")

Musset's fifth principle, then, is the thematic priority of love within the realm of self-expression. And within the thematics of love, it is love's sad consequences that Musset will stress; this is part of Musset's originality within the tradition of the love lyric. He subscribes to the romantic dogma, expounded from Mme de Staël to Baudelaire, that grief is the most profound, the most "philosophical" of man's emotions: "Une larme est ce qu'il y a de plus vrai, de plus impérissable au monde" (*Oeuvres complètes en prose*, p. 331)

> Le seul bien qui me reste au monde
> Est d'avoir quelquefois pleuré.
> ("Tristesse")

> Rien ne nous rend si grands qu'une grande douleur.
> (*La Nuit de Mai*)

It follows— and this is his sixth principle— that the greater the grief the greater the poem. Like Shelley he believes that our sweetest songs are those that tell of saddest thoughts.

> Les plus désespérés sont les chants les plus beaux,
> Et j'en sais d'immortels qui sont de purs sanglots.
> (Ibid.)

A seventh principle: poetry is not emotion recollected in tranquility; it is emotion translated at the very moment of crisis or paroxysm. It is not a craft, it is a *cri de coeur* uttered in a state of nervous tension.

> Au moment du travail, chaque nerf, chaque fibre,
> Tressaille comme un luth que l'on vient d'accorder.
> On n'écrit pas un mot que tout l' être ne vibre.
> (Soit dit sans vanité, c'est ce que l'on ressent.)
> On ne travaille pas, —on écoute, — on attend.
> C'est comme un inconnu qui vous parle à voix basse.
> On reste quelquefois une nuit sur la place,
> Sans faire un mouvement et sans se retourner.
> ("Dédicace" to La Coupe et les Lèvres)

> Sachez-le— c'est le coeur qui parle et qui soupire
> Lorsque la main écrit, —c'est le coeur qui se fond;
> C'est le coeur qui s'étend, se découvre et respire. . . .
> (Namouna)

Musset subscribes to Chénier's dictum: "L'art ne fait que des vers, le coeur seul est poète." And he would certainly have approved of Robert Grave's distinction between "verse rhetoric, the product of cold reason, and true poetry, the result of an emotional trance" (quoted by M. Rees, *Musset*, p. 60). When he says in "Après une lecture:" "Mon premier point sera qu'il faut déraisonner," he means that the poet should present the emotion *toute chaude* and not cooled by intellectual reformulations and artistic calculation.

Note, before we proceed, that we are talking here of Musset's poetics, *not* his poetry. His actual, finished poems are only initially inspired by an intense emotional experience; they are then chiseled—whether carefully or casually [and often Musset's casualness is a matter of ironic tonality, that is, a studied casualness] —into a work of art. This will become clearer in the second part of this chapter when we explore the role of ideas in Musset's conception of the poetic function.

Musset's poetics is superficially related to Plato's "sacred fury" and the ideas on poetic inspiration expounded by the poets of the Pléiade. But "inspiration" for Musset is not a question of divine afflatus; it is Experience that provides the sacred spark. To sing one must have something to sing about, one must have lived intensely. It is of this intensity that he speaks and not poetic madness in the following line—

> Les heureux sont les fous; les poètes le sont.
> ("A Ninon")

Musset believes in the primacy, the logical priority of life over art. If poetry is self-expression, the poet must first have an interesting self to express. He would agree with Russell in Joyce's *Ulysses*: "The supreme question about a work of art is out of how deep a life does it spring."

La Nuit d'Octobre adds an eighth principle to Musset's poetics: poetry as consolation and catharsis, that is, its healing powers. Suffering teaches self-knowledge, compassion, the appreciation of life's rare moments of joy; and by articulating his grief the poet finds consolation and is purged of bitterness and guilt.

> En se plaignant on se console.
> Et quelquefois une parole
> Nous a delivrés d'un remords.

The Muse of *La Nuit de Mai* had already said: "Ah! je t'ai consolé d'une amère souffrance!" The idea is repeated in a lighter vein in "Après une lecture:"

> A nous autres, rimeurs, de qui la grande affaire
> Est de nous consoler en arrangeant des mots. . .

But his is not just a poetics of self-expression and self deliverance. His public, which we wants large, will identify with the intense emotions described so directly, so spontaneously and sincerely, and will enlarge its own experience through vicarious suffering (and, occasionally, joy).

> Vive le mélodrame où Margot a pleuré!
>
> . . .
>
> Margot s'y connaît.
> ("Après une lecture")

This *boutade* expresses Musset's conviction that the poet does not write for himself alone or for an elite, the happy few. In "Les Voeux stériles" he proclaims: "Point d'*arrière aux profanes*" And he writes in the "Salon de 1836" that there is no greater error in the arts than to believe in spheres too elevated for the layman: "Il faut chercher à attirer la foule, à être compris et aimé par elle" (*Oeuvres complètes*, p. 859).

> Etre admiré n'est rien, l'affaire est d'être aimé
> ("Après une lecture")

He believes ("Salon de 1836") that the work of art lives on two conditions:

the first is to please the crowd, and the second to please the connoisseurs at the very same time. There is something more than a *boutade*, then, in the following lines from the prologue to *Les Marrons du feu*

> La pièce, à parler franc, est digne de Molière;
> Qui le pourrait nier? Mon groom et ma portière,
> Qui l'ont lue, en ont été contents.

and in *Namouna*, when he alludes to Molière's servant:

> Ah! pauvre Laforêt, qui ne savait pas lire. . .
> Il ne te lisait pas, dit-on, les vers d'Alceste;
> Si je les avais faits, je te les aurais lus.

The impact of a poem on the general public is the poet's main reward and the touchstone of true poetry.

> Pourquoi donc les amants veillent-ils nuit et jour?
> Pourquoi donc le poète aime-t-il sa souffrance?
> Que demandent-ils donc tous les deux en retour?
> Une larme, ô mon Dieu, voilà leur récompense;
> Voilà pour eux le ciel, la gloire et l'éloquence,
> Et par là le génie est semblable à l'amour.
> (*Namouna*)

The word *larme* does not express the poet's desire to be pitied, but, rather, to produce a *shared* emotion. The extreme importance that Musset attaches to his audience, indeed to a wide audience, means that the final goal is not self-expression but the poet's sharing of his most intimate experience with his readers. The exposure of his deepest wounds is the poet's supreme task and his supreme sacrifice, an idea expressed, again, in the parable of the pelican. Self-expression provides the subject-matter, but the ultimate goal, we might call it the final principle of his poetics, is communication, or better, communion.

*
* *

2. The Role of Ideas

Despite the great importance of emotion there is more to Musset's poetics than an *esthétique du sentiment*. Ideas play a crucial role in Musset's conception of the poetic experience, as revealed in two significant but little known texts that compel a reassessment of the comfortable clichés that have held Musset's poetics in the pigeonhole of "poetry as *épanchement*."

The first text is from *Le Poète déchu*:

> Le poète n'écrit jamais la réflexion; le prosateur n'est juste et profond que par elle. Le poète cependant doit la sentir et plus profondément encore que le prosateur, par cette raison que pour exprimer *son idée*, quelle qu'elle soit et n'importe comment, quand ce ne serait que pour la rime, il faut qu'il travaille longtemps. Or, pendant ce travail obligé, une multitude de commentaires, de faces diverses, de corollaires sont plus ou moins bons, brillants, justes, séduisants; ils détournent, ramènent, expliquent, enchantent; pour le prosateur, ce sont des veines, des minerais; pour le poète, les reflets d'un prisme.
>
> Il faut au poète le jet de l'âme, *l'idée mère*; il s'y attache, et cependant peut-il résoudre à perdre le fruit de sa réflexion? S'il n'a que quatre lignes à écrire, il faut donc que le reste y entre; de là ce qu'on nomme *la poésie, c'est-à-dire ce qui fait penser*. Dans tout vers remarquable d'un vrai poète, il y a deux ou trois fois plus que ce qui est dit; c'est au lecteur à suppléer le reste, selon ses *idées*, sa force, ses goûts.
>
> (*OEuvres complètes*, p. 650; our emphasis)

This passage is more suggestive than explicit and requires some interpretation. One can construct from it a coherent statement, in fact one that is not out of line with current semiotic thinking about the nature of the poetic text. I am thinking in particular here of the ideas of Michael Riffaterre as expressed in his *Semiotics of Poetry* and *La Production du texte*. Here is what Musset is saying when we put some new words in his mouth.

Poetry is not discursive thought but *produces* thought. It begins with a "deeply felt" idea (the *idée mère*: the matrix or invariant structure which, while unspoken and outside the text— "Le poète n'écrit jamais la réflexion"— will engender the text) and it ends in still other ideas (the reactions and rationalizations of the reader).

The controlling idea is "deeply felt" not just because of the original emotional experience but because the poet is "obliged" to work under the constraints of genre, of prosody, and the demands of high quality, to use carefully words and the ideas they form in working out the specifics of his larger design: "pour exprimer son idée. . . il faut qu'il travaille longtemps." The role of emotion is crucial in Musset's poetics; he will stress it as the *source* of his poetry; but when the poet puts pen to paper, the moment inspiration becomes creation, the role of emotion is *already over*: it has allowed (or forced) the poet to select his *idée mère*. The *coeur qui parle* hyperbole, which Musset's critics have taken literally, is misleading: the "heart" plays its most important role *before*, not during the creative performance. Musset is not naive: he knows perfectly well that a poem is composed of words, of signs, not sentiments.

The "corollaires" are the variants of the invariant "deep structure", the network of associated ideas which, if used, will be expressed by *signifiants* that refer only indirectly to *signifiés* or referents outside the text and directly to each other (those *reflets d'un prisme*, the "various facets" of the crystalline poetic structure that reflect each other.) Musset's prism reflections anticipate structuralist-semiotic pronouncements on the essence of the poem. One thinks of Jakobson's characterization of the poetic function: the referential function of language is replaced by the reference to the form, to the poem itself; and Riffaterre: "Le poème est un énoncé qui se reflète soi-même; une forme est à peine donnée qu'elle produit son synonyme ou son contraire" (*Production du texte*, p. 215). The poet in elaborating tautologically the *idée mère* condenses and suggests corollary ideas ("il faut que le reste y entre.") Note the emphasis on suggestiveness ("Dans tout vers remarquable. . . il y a deux ou trois fois plus que ce qui est dit") in Musset's poetics, a trait that links his to "modernist" theories, and also the phenomenological bent: "c'est au lecteur à suppléer le reste." It is the role of the poet to stir the mind as well as the "heart" of his reader, *faire penser*; this could be taken as the first principle (or, as we suggested earlier, the last, since it expresses the final goal) of his poetics, communication or communion. It is the role of the reader, according to his linguistic and literary "competence" ("selon ses idées, sa force, ses goûts") to connect the literary signs to each other and to what is not directly stated, to the "rest, " to the *non-dit*.

Pierre Reboul and Patricia Siegel are the only critics writing on Musset up to now who have seen the importance of thought in his poetics. Reboul writes: "Mais il dit aussi, au prix d'un faux sens, que [la poésie] *fait penser*. Qu'elle est *pensée*. Que, dans les affres et les atermoiements de l'enfantement, le poète ne peut pas ne pas penser; que son *texte* conserve la trace de tous ces "corollaires" non énoncés, de toutes ces intentions

62

avortées, d'un *non dit* qui l'auréole. Ecrire, c'est, à la fois, avoir pensé et faire penser ("Le Poète...", p. 156). Musset's "corollaires," however, should not be equated with aborted intentions. They are, again, all the relevant associated ideas, some of which will find their way directly into the text, others which will only be hinted at or which will be omitted entirely according to the needs of the developing context.

For Musset there seem to be four distinct stages in the total poetic experience.

1. *émotion*	2. *idée mère*	3. *poème*	4. *pensée*
the original emotional experience, crucial for the poem's genesis, but not its semiosis.	the conversion of the experience into an idea that will serve as the nucleus of the poem. The poet is ready to compose, to turn experience into discourse.	the finished product for the poet, but *point de départ* (Riffaterre) for the reader.	the end result: the reader's reaction, his emotional *and* intellectual response to the elaborated *idée mère* (the poem) based on "l'input da sa mythologie" (*Production du texte*, p. 154)

Let us now look at an oft-quoted statement of Musset on the importance of emotion, putting it, however, within the proper framework: the four-stage process outlined above.

> Ce qu'il faut à l'artiste ou au poète, c'est l'émotion. Quand j'éprouve, en faisant un vers, un certain battement de coeur que je connais, je suis sûr que mon vers est de la meilleure qualité que je puisse pondre" (*Correspondance*, p. 27)

The first sentence seems to be referring to the poem's genesis, stage one. But the main sentence clearly indicates that Musset is thinking of stage four: the poet is trying out his product on himself, as *reader*. His emotional response is a litmus test of the poem's "quality," but the response was not elicited from a vacuum, it is the result of the poet's successful elaboration of the *idée mère*. What triggers the reader's emotional response to a poem is not a raw emotion but a carefully articulated and thus intellectualized emotion within a well wrought artifact. Moreover, the reader's response is a vicarious and intellectualized response, produced by and mediated through signs.

*
* *

The second text is Musset's "Impromptu" of 1839.

EN RÉPONSE À CETTE QUESTION: QU'EST-CE QUE LA POÉSIE?

Chasser tout souvenir et fixer la *pensée*,
Sur un bel axe d'or la tenir balancée,
Incertaine, inquiète, immobile pourtant;
Eterniser peut-être un rêve d'un instant;
Aimer le vrai, le beau, chercher leur harmonie;
Ecouter dans son coeur, l'écho de son génie;
Chanter, rire, pleurer, seul, sans but, au hasard;
D'un sourire, d'un mot, d'un soupir, d'un regard
Faire un travail exquis, plein de crainte et de charme,
   Faire une perle d'une larme:
D'un poète ici-bas voilà la passion,
Voilà son bien, sa vie et son ambition.

This text too is of signal importance when one is trying to understand Musset's poetics *as a whole*. It is the only other one in which he reconciles emotion with thought and shows that they are not antagonistic but complementary elements of poetry. The first line presents an ambiguous antithesis: *souvenir* in this context refers to fleeting, superficial memories of significant experiences, experiences that will be forever lost if not converted by art into objects of contemplation ("pensée"). Emotion ("chanter, rire, pleurer;" "son coeur") is the starting point; the poem (the pearl) is the finished product, carefully wrought ("D'un sourire. . . d'un soupir faire un travail exquis"). The poet's "passion and ambition" is to capture meaningful experience ("le vrai"), to convert it into poetic discourse ("le beau;" "leur harmonie") and thus into lasting thought ("pensée. . . immobile;" "éterniser un rêve d'un moment").

Emotion is thus converted into *intellectual* beauty. The poet, again, is not naive: he knows full well that a poem is not pretty to look at, that the sounds of the most euphonious poem do not produce an aesthetic experience without the sense, that the poetical image of an emotion is not the emotion itself. Indeed, art is artifact; all literary signs are designs. Art makes its own demands on emotional experience, and so does every page of every text, every line of every poem. "Pour exprimer son idée. . . il faut qu'il travaille longtemps:" This statement, although not as dogmatic or insistent, is not so far removed from Gautier's injunction:

> Sculpte, lime, cisèle;
> Que ton rêve flottant
> Se scelle
> Dans le bloc résistant!

And the entire "Impromptu" could have been worked into Gautier's *ars poetica*. The "rêve flottant" corresponds exactly to Musset's "rêve d'un moment;" and the verb *se scelle* is echoed in Musset's *éterniser*.

Musset begins, then, by reacting deeply—"depth" for him means intense emotional reactions *and* intellectual or spiritual reverberations—to the most meaningful experiences of his life; but the meaningfulness can be captured only in an idea, and an idea can be fully expressed only with words; only words can generalize, intellectualize and distill (spiritualize) the essence of life as it is lived concretely, materially and inarticulately. If the poet is successful, if he has made a tear into a pearl, as Musset has compellingly expressed it, he has accomplished what another writer has called man's supreme task as a human being: to convert matter into spirit.

chapter four
MUSSET'S POETIC WORLD:
A TREMBLING UNIVERSE
IN PERPETUAL MOTION

O mon ami! le monde incessamment remue/Autour de nous, en nous. . .
                    (*Suzon*)

Quelle agitation, quel bruit dans la cité!
Quel monstre remuant que cette humanité!
                    (*La Coupe et les Lèvres*)

. . . Notre esprit inconstant
Se prend de fantaisie et vit de changement.
                    ("A la Mi-Carême")

Sais-je, au moment où je te quitte,
Où m'entraîne mon astre errant?
Je m'en vais pourtant, ma petite,
    Bien loin, bien vite, Toujours courant.
                    ("Adieux à Suzon")

Je me sauve en tremblant de la réalité.
                    ("Stances")

Musset,"cerf-volant," and "Prince Phosphore-de-coeur-volant," was a
man of unstable temperament, of quicksilver moods, of fickle fancies
and contradictory impulses, a man divided and always on the run.
Wavering constantly between idealism and cynicism, he yearned for true
love and for an enduring faith, but just as constant were his *méfiance*
and his unbelief. Vague religiosity and anguished incredulity were to
follow him side by side throughout his life. Changeability was his essence:
nothing could hold his attention for long. The frightful vulture, Boredom,
he said, had early marked him as its prey. Epicurean delights, the
excitements of wine, women, song and gambling, even the blessed
moments of poetic inspiration—all were quickly and inevitably followed
by periods of let-down, of *abattement*. His "instinct for unhappiness,"
as he called it, caused the sweetest honey that touched his lips to change
to bitter brew.

Musset himself was painfully aware of the contradictions in his nature.
He speaks in his correspondence of the two totally different men that
inhabit him. In one passage it is the man of action and the passive observer,
in another it is the idealist and the cynic, Coelio and Octave. His

biographers have spoken of the Chérubin-Don Juan antinomy and of Jeckell and Hyde. Madame Allan-Despréaux says of him: "I have never seen a more striking contrast than the two beings contained in this one person. One is good, gentle, tender, enthusiastic, full of wit and common sense, naive. . . If you turn the page and look on the other side, you find a man possessed by a sort of devil. . . His nature consists of extremes, both good and bad" (quoted by M. Rees, *Musset*, p. 31). A psychoanalytically oriented biographer, Pierre Odoul (*Le drame intime*, pp. 76-77 and 175), speaks of Musset's strong Id, especially the dominance of the pleasure principle, constantly countered by a strong super-ego (unconscious emulation of his highly moral parents). Morality and libertinage, modesty and impertinence, sociability and solitariness, gaiety and moroseness cohabited in him and fought for dominance. They were all unsuccessful, the battle being internecine.

The inner conflict that troubled him most was that between his yearning for ideal, pure love and his incapacity to achieve it or even believe in it fully. Odoul, somewhat gratuitously, finds the trouble in a mother-fixation (Sand being six years older, Mme Jaubert being the *marraine*, etc.) that becomes a sister-fixation. Others have pointed to his inveterate masochism. Here, the internal evidence of Musset's literary work is convincing, as a small sampling illustrates.

> Et cependant mon coeur prit un amer plaisir
> A sentir qu'il aimait et qu'il allait souffrir!
> > ("Idylle")

> Rien n'est bon que d'aimer, n'est vrai que de souffrir.
> > (*A la Malibran*)

> Et que d'amour de vous il est doux de souffrir!
> > . . .
> Et que le tourment même est une volupté!
> > ("A Ninon")

Love is called a "douleur chérie" in "A Ninon," a "délicieuse souffrance" in *Carmosine*. Then there is the medallion bearing the portrait of his mistress that the autobiographical Octave of the *Confession d'un enfant du siècle* turns into an instrument of masochistic pleasure:

> Je le portais sur le coeur, chose que font bien des hommes; mais, ayant trouvé un jour chez un marchand de curiosités une discipline de fer, au bout de laquelle était une plaque hérissée de pointes, j'avais fait attacher le médaillon sur la plaque et

le portais ainsi. Ces clous, qui m'entraient dans la poitrine à
chaque mouvement, me causaient une volupté si étrange que
j'appuyais quelque fois ma main pour les sentir plus
profondément.

(OEuvres complètes, p. 564)

Whatever the unconscious springs of his amorous behavior and
misbehavior, his conscious efforts to achieve a lasting love were always
frustrated.

His brother Paul has spoken of the "mobility" of Musset's mind; Sainte-
Beuve, who knew him well, has said: "Avec Musset tout se menait vite
et courait" (Causeries, 13, p. 370); and Mme Jaubert, who knew him
even better, says of him: "Il n'est pas de ciel orageux, panaché, éclairé
par un soleil de mars, dont la mobilité puisse être comparée à celle de
son humeur" (quoted by Emile Henriot (Musset, p. 103). Both Sainte-
Beuve and Maurice Toesca have noticed the acceleration of seasons in
Musset's life.

> Que ne prenait-il patience? Tout serait venu en sa saison.
> Mais il avait hâte de condenser et de dévorer les saisons. (quoted
> by Gauthier-Ferrières, Musset, p. 99)

> Il y a eu chez Musset un décalage constant dans les saisons
> de son existence: enfant, il s'imagine adolescent, et il l'est en
> réalité pour sa culture; vers la quinzième année. . . il a déjà
> lu tant et tant de livres qu'il est gonflé de poésie, de rêves,
> d'aventures, de désirs qui sont ceux d'un adulte. (L'Amour de
> la mort, p. 41)

Musset's precocity and impatience made of him a romantic puer senex,
older (but not wiser) than his years. Jean Pommier has distinguished
between normal human time and "le temps de Musset:" "Tout est emporté
à un rythme différent du nôtre" (Musset, p. 8). To observe Musset's psyche
is to observe restless, rapid movements.

> Je vais et viens, j'avance et je recule: un instinct singulier
> me pousse et m'attire. Je ne sais si c'est de peur ou de plaisir
> que je frissonne.
> (Correspondance, p. 72)

> Où me mène donc cette main invisible qui ne veut pas que
> je m'arrête? (Ibid., p. 67)

> Tergiversant, tournoyant, débraillé . . . c'est ma parfaite
> image. (Ibid., p. 184)

There are movements of impulsiveness, impetuousness and impatience; movements too of excited anticipation and movements of remorse. Other movements arise from his near manic-depressive swings in mood, his constant shuttlings between contradictory patterns of behavior—jerky movements, then, caused by unstable equilibrium. His well documented masochism is a voluntary return to the scene of the pain; here the movement is cyclical: "Son cycle idéal: sortir de l'ennui par la conquête passionnelle, en souffrir, chanter sa douleur pour s'en libérer, puis retomber finalement dans l'ennui" (Toesca, pp. 199-200) There are centrifugal movements away from the norm and toward the extremes: "J'ai besoin d'un excès quelconque" (*Correspondance*, p. 15). There are movements away from the real and toward the impossible: George Sand has spoken in *Elle et Lui* of Musset's love of what does not exist. This is the constant movement of the eternal questor, which in the poetry is expressed by a variety of analogous images: the eagle flying toward (but not reaching) the high mountain top, the miner digging furiously for diamonds in the bowels of the earth, the diver sinking deeper and deeper in the unplumbed depths, the traveler who feels the ground beneath him collapse as soon as he arrives, Don Juan on his "infinite road" seeking an "être impossible," Frank pushing ever forward toward an ever-receding goal.

> Tout le porte, l'entraîne à son but idéal,
> Clarté toujours fuyant, et toujours poursuivie.[1]

There are movements of aversion, even from happiness: "Au bal, dans les réunions et les fêtes riantes, quand il rencontrait le plaisir, il ne s'y tenait pas, il cherchait par la réflexion à en tirer tristesse, amertume. . . (Sainte-Beuve, *Causeries*, 13, p. 366). This strange gift, or handicap, for seeing the worm the moment he bites into the fruit, of seeing the slip 'twixt the cup and the lip (*La Coupe et les Lèvres* is his most philosophical play), has led Pierre Gastinel to speak of his contractile movements, his *contractilité*. Other critics, Charlotte Dolder (*Etre et paraître*, pp. 21 and 135) and Jean-Pierre Richard have seen oscillating and undulating movements as both the poet and the man shuttle between opposite moods and impulses: "Il oscille sans cesse sur lui-même, passe brusquement d'un parti au parti opposé. . . hésitation, atermoiement, volte-face imprévue: c'est la loi de cet univers déboussolé" (Richard, *Etudes*, p. 209). Philippe Soupault has summed him up well as the poet of vertigo.

The mobility of his temperament no doubt influenced his general outlook on life, which is characterized by the mobility and changeability he sees in all things human and inhuman. His "bien suprême" was love, *l'amour-passion*. But love, like all of Nature's creations is subject to her first law, the law of impermanence, inconstancy and inevitable change. Man is a creature inherently incapable of sustaining the intensity of a deep passion. He is both the victim and the agent of change. His cynical Don Juans—Rafaël, Mardoche, Hassan—change mistresses nearly as often as they change their clothes. His idealistic Don Juans are also subject to the law of impermanence. The Don Juan of *Namouna* goes from woman to woman in search of what Drieu la Rochelle's Gille calls "cette créature tout à fait réussie." He sacrifices his physical and spiritual energy in search of an impossible dream. Musset's other idealistic Don Juan, the hero of *La Matinée de Don Juan*, asks himself: "et que te reste-t-il pour avoir voulu te désaltérer tant de fois? — Une soif ardente, ô mon Dieu!" (*OEuvres complètes*, p. 496). The movements of all his Don Juans, then, resemble those found in all the great myths of frustration—Sisyphus, Axion, the Danaïdes, Tantalus—the movements of an eternal treadmill.

Love can arise from the ashes through the persistence of memory: The privileged moments live on in memory, in poetry and in the soul's immortal consciousness (*Lettre à Lamartine; Souvenir*). But privileged moments are fleeting by nature and rare by definition. It is the law of change that remains primary in Musset's view of reality. The inexorability of change governs not only love but friendship, worldly glory, politics and history. The death of a celebrated singer (La Malibran) becomes a forgotten story in a fortnight. Politicians change with the wind and their conflicting ideas are quickly adopted and abandoned by a fickle populace. It is the latter who is blamed for the confusing acceleration of history since 1789.

> De tant de jours de deuil, de crainte et d'espérance,
> De tant d'efforts perdus, de tant de maux soufferts,
> En es-tu lasse enfin, pauvre terre de France?
> Et de tes vieux enfants l'éternelle inconstance
> Laissera-t-elle un jour de calme à l'univers?
>
> Comprends-tu tes destins et sais-tu ton histoire?
> Depuis un demi-siècle as-tu compté tes pas?
> Est-ce assez de grandeur, de misère et de gloire,
> Et, sinon par pitié pour ta propre mémoire,
> Par fatigue du moins t'arrêteras-tu pas?
> ("Sur la naissance du Conte de Paris")

To the law of impermanence and change must be added the second law of emotional dynamics in Musset's *univers déboussolé*: entropy.

Change moves in one direction only: from a higher order to a lower one; from paroxysm to apathy and boredom. All the good things in life—hopes, dreams, ideals, love—wear down and wear out.

> La première expérience, Aimée, consiste à souffrir, elle consiste à trouver et à sentir que les rêves absolus ne se réalisent presque jamais; ou que réalisés, ils se flétrissent et meurent au contact des choses de ce monde.
> (*Lettres d'Amour*, p. 59)

> Les liens de ce monde, même les plus forts se dénouent la plupart du temps. (*OEuvres complètes*, p. 715)

> Ce noir torrent qui mène tout à rien. ("Sur la paresse")

> Il faut que tout s'évanouisse. ("Silvia")

> Tout s'en va comme la fumée. (*Le Saule*)

> Tout meurt. (*Souvenir*)

> Tout s'use. (*Mardoche*)

Musset's universe is in constant flux too because it is ruled not by providential Necessity

> Nous n'avons pas du moins cette sotte pensée
> De croire que le monde ait été fait pour nous.
> ("Brandel")

but by Chance, "l'inconstant hasard." "La Providence donne le hasard" is the epigraph, from Schiller, that he gives to *Portia*. In the "Réponse à M. Charles Nodier" the poet describes himself as a "child adopted and spoiled by Chance." In his early youth he did indeed pose as the spoiled and insouciant dandy who was quite willing to let Chance dictate his whims.

> Sortir seul au hasard, chantant quelque refrain.
> ("Après une lecture")

> Puis j'allais par hasard au théâtre en fumant.
> ("Une bonne fortune")

But in his maturity he came to curse "l'instabilité des choses d'ici-bas et les impitoyables caprices du hasard" (*OEuvres complètes*, p. 730). It is with bitterness that Frank, Musset's most philosophical hero, calls himself "fils du hasard." The word *hasard* occurs much too frequently in Musset's work to be dismissed as a facile filler.

Le hasard voulut que ce lieu
Fût au penchant d'une prairie.
("Simone")

. . . ceux dont le hasard couronna la naissance.
("Au Roi")

Un vers presque inconnu, refrain inachevé,
Frais comme le hasard.
("Une soirée perdue")

Le hasard peut tout.
(*Namouna*)

Là, du soir au matin, roule le grand *peut-être*,
Le hasard, noir flambeau de ces siècles d'ennui,
Le seul qui dans le ciel flotte encore aujourd'hui.
("Une bonne fortune")

Maintenant le hasard premène au sein des ombres
De leurs illusions les mondes réveillés.
(*Rolla*)

La poussière est à Dieu. — Le reste est au hasard.
(*La Coupe*)

Indeed Paul de Musset tells us in the Biography that the vision of a universe ruled by capricious Chance had become a veritable obsession with his brother. Even in his most religious poem Musset will complain: "Dans la création le hasard m'a jeté" (*L'Espoir en Dieu*).

*

* *

This view of a universe governed by chance and change is reflected in Musset's style: the quickly changing tonalities, the contradictory moods, the sudden switching of themes, the mixing of registers, the shifting perspectives, the romantic irony, the tendency to juxtapose fragments—in short the centrifugal structures enumerated in chapter two.

Musset's imagery is informed by this vision of a fragile, volatile, constantly moving and trembling world. People are compared to blades of grass (grass itself is seen as "running" in "A la Mi-Carême" and "Simone"), to thin reeds, to grains of sand, to ashes, dust, smoke, the changing tide. The verbs (*s'*)*agiter, branler, chanceller, fléchir, frémir, frémisser, frissonner, remuer, secouer, tourner, tournoyer, trébucher, trembler, tressaillir* recur over and over in his narrative and dramatic poetry to portray the actions and reactions of his heroes and heroines and, in his lyric poetry, of himself and his personae. His young protagonists tremble in the anticipation, the enjoyment or the recollection of passion; or from the premonition of their partner's infidelity; or in the commission of a crime of passion; often it is from inebriation, the risks at the gambling table or the throes or mere thought of premature death. Since the Revolution all of France "staggers," he says, from having drunk too quickly and too deeply of Freedom and from the loss of its greatest man, the Emperor. The cross of Christ "trembles" from the onslought of Voltaire and his fellow *démolisseurs*; the Holy Ghost, mortally wounded dove, falls fitfully, twisting and turning, out of control, into the abyss of eternal oblivion.

> Pour qui travailliez-vous, démolisseurs stupides,
> Lorsque vous disséquiez le Christ sur son autel?
> Que vouliez-vous semer sur sa céleste tombe,
> Quand vous jetiez au vent la sanglante colombe,
> Qui tombe en tournoyant dans l'abîme éternel.
> *(Rolla)*

The skeptical poet himself "trembles" more than once before the eternal silence of infinite space.

Another of Musset's favorite verbs is *voltiger* because, says Pierre Moreau ("L'Ironie de Musset," p. 506) of the capricious movements it evokes. It occurs throughout his poetry but especially of course in the bird imagery. Musset's birds are not feathered songsters perched contentedly on a still bough but birds on the wing (see M. Herschensohn, "Imagery. . . in Musšet," p. 66). Whether the bird in a particular context is associated with a yearning for happiness or, as with the frequently recurring swallows, with the end of happiness, it is usually a bird in movement.

> Où va l'homme? Où son coeur l'appelle.
> L'hirondelle suit le zéphyr,
> Et moins légère est l'hirondelle
> Que l'homme qui suit son désir.
> ("Chanson")
>
> Ou, comme en soupirant l'hirondelle s'envole
> Mon bonheur fuira-t-il, n'ayant duré qu'un soir?
> ("A quoi rêvent. . .")
>
> Vous qui volez là-bas, légères hirondelles,
> Dites-moi, dites-moi, pourquoi vais-je mourir?
> *(Rolla)*

Le temps emporte sur son aile
Et le printemps et l'hirondelle,
Et la vie et les jours perdus. . .
                ("A Juana")

The swallow represents swift movement, fragility, change of season and state, evanescence leading to death. These associations are traditional, but the choice of image and the frequency of the choice are significant.

Musset's use of liquid imagery and his images of light and of night derive from the same psychological impulses and philosophical biases. Michael Herschensohn has studied Musset's water imagery from a phenomenological viewpoint and has found that in all of it there appears to be motion of some kind. He concludes that "Musset's view of life can be conceived of as motion, as a wave whose curve can readily plotted on a graph" ("Imagery in Musset," p. 66). Simon Jeune ("Aspects. . ." p. 184) has noted that in Musset's images of light there is always something uncertain and trembling. James Hewitt ("Tropes of Self," chapter one) has studied Musset's nocturnal imagery and found that the Mussetian night is not one of repose but rather a feverish, sleepless night, one of uncontrolled passion or impending fatality: *folles nuits, nuits sans sommeil, nuits d'insomnie.*

*

* *

The fact that Musset's imaginative universe is a trembling one is confirmed by an examination of his fictional and theatrical work. In *La Confession d'un enfant du siècle*, in his autobiographical *nouvelles* and in his more serious plays, his heroes and leading ladies tremble physically as well as figuratively with each new emotional experience and in every part of their body: hands, arms, feet, voice, heart, shoulders. [Musset himself was frequently seized with convulsive tremblings of the face and neck, tremblings that became more violent in his later years.] Often it is the whole body that trembles. The verb *trembler* recurs with the same high frequency as in the poetry and, as in the poetry, is frequently reinforced by *frémir, frissonner, tressaillir* and half a dozen other synonyms. This stylistic tic can be attributed only in part to romantic hyperbole (or, more accurately, to a throwback to eighteenth-century *sensibilité*); more significantly it reflects the genuine hypersensitivity that Musset's protagonists share with their creator. For his fictional and dramatic heroes disorder is the order of the day, inconstancy the only constant in their behavior. The reader or spectator can become almost dizzy from the rapidity of change he observes in Musset's leading characters. At the end of *La Nuit vénitienne*, for example, Razetta will move from utter despair to insouciant gaiety in—literally—a matter of seconds. The dissipated Octave of *Les Caprices de Marianne* boasts that he will not spill one drop from his cup of joy on the tight rope he walks through life, but admits he must move "faster than the wind" to keep his balance. The verb *trembler* and its synonyms are used 73 times by my count in Musset's plays, eight times in *Le Chandelier* alone and fifteen times in *Lorenzaccio*.

Musset's fictional heroes are as unstable as his theatrical protagonists. They are incapable of assuming a career (Octave, Prévan [the narrator-hero of *Le Roman par lettres*] and Pippo [*Le Fils de Titien*]); they often exhibit dual personalities (Octave and Valentin, hero of *Les deux maîtresses*, of whom the narrator says: "Ce fut ainsi qu'il devint double et qu'il vécut en perpétuelle contradiction avec lui-même" (*OEuvres complètes*, p. 654); they possess inconstant tastes and desires (Prévan, Pippo and the hero of *Le Poète déchu* who says of himself: "Mon esprit mobile et curieux tremble incessamment comme la boussole" [ibid., p. 648]).

Inconstancy and instability are often presented in Musset's fiction not only as the essence of his heroes but of mankind in general; they are even seen to be in the very nature of "things."

> Comme vous êtes homme et inconstant vous-même
> (*La Confession*)

> Il n'y a rien de stable ici-bas. (Ibid)

> Les liens de ce monde, même les plus forts, se dénouent la plupart du temps. (*Frédéric et Bernerette*)

> L'inconstance des choses. . . (Ibid)

> L'instabilité des choses d'ici-bas. . . (*Margot*)

Musset is the only major French dramatist of the nineteenth century to write under the modern assumption that psychological truth is elusive and unstable. Life is called a dream (*La Nuit vénitienne; Caprices*), a shadow (*Caprices*), a stormy sea, a slippery soil and a precipice (*Lorenzaccio.*), a pun (*Fantasio*), and a pantomime (*La Quenouille de Barberine*) in which the gestures have nothing to do with the thought or spoken word. Human emotions are presented as incoherent and contradictory, ambiguous and ambivalent, constantly changing without rhyme or reason. To say that a man is good or bad, happy or unhappy, is folly.

> La gaîté est quelquefois triste, et la mélancolie a le sourire sur les lèvres. (*Andre del Sarto*)

> Votre gaieté est triste comme la nuit. (*Lorenzaccio*)

ELSBETH: Tu me fais l'effet de regarder le monde à travers un prisme tant soit peu changeant.

FANTASIO: Chacun a ses lunettes; mais personne ne sait au juste de quelle couleur en sont les verres. Qui est-ce qui pourra me dire au juste si je suis heureux ou malheureux, bon ou mauvais, triste ou gai, bête ou spirituel. (*Fantasio*)

Human behavior is governed neither by inner nor external necessity. "Je parle beaucoup au hasard," puns Fantasio, "c'est mon plus cher confident." Capriciousness is found not only in the heroine of *Les Caprices de Marianne* but in the plot itself. In fact at one point in the play Octave widens the application of capriciousness to metaphysical dimensions: "La justice céleste tient une balance dans ses mains. . . mais tous les poids sont creux. . . et toutes les actions humaines s'en vont de haut en bas, selon ces poids capricieux." Pierre Gastinel has said that all of Musset's plays could be entitled *Les Caprices de* . . .

*
* *

At times, Musset's vision of a trembling world is truly cosmic in scope. His world, not just the terrestrial realm of human relationships but the entire physical universe, is in constant motion, and it is love, or rather the yearning for love (physical desire) that literally makes this mobile world go round.

In *La Confession* he speaks of love as a *loi céleste* equal in power and incomprehensibility to the law of gravity. In a striking and surprising development of this thought he changes the status of this "celestial" law from the figurative to the literal: Love becomes his *explanation* of the law of gravity; it becomes the central law of celestial mechanics. Human love is now but a local manifestation of the law of universal attraction that keeps the entire cosmos in motion.

Pourquoi le ciel immense n'est-il pas immobile? Dites-moi s'il y a jamais eu un moment où tout fut créé. En vertu de quelle force ont-ils commencé à se mouvoir, ces mondes qui ne s'arrêteront jamais? . . . Par l'éternel amour. La plus faible d'entre les étoiles s'est élancée vers l'astre qu'elle adore comme son bien-aimée; mais une autre l'aimait elle-même, et l'univers s'est mis en voyage.

This idea was so important to Musset that he expressed it both in *Le Roman par lettres* and *Il ne faut jurer de rien* and in exactly the same terms. The thought is also expressed in *Rolla*.

J'aime!—voilà le mot que la nature entière
Crie au vent qui l'emporte, à l'oiseau qui le suit!
Sombre et dernier soupir que poussera la terre
Quand elle tombera dans l'éternelle nuit!
Oh! vous le murmurez dans vos sphères sacrées,
Etoiles du matin, ce mot triste et charmant!
La plus faible de vous, quand Dieu vos a créées,
A voulu traverser les plaines éthérées,
Pour chercher le soleil, son immortel amant.
Elle s'est élancée au sein des nuits profondes.
Mais une autre l'aimait elle-même; et les mondes
Se sont mis en voyage autour du firmament.

Maurice Allem's comment on this passage is germane: "Alfred de Musset tient, on le voit, à cette interprétation symbolique de la loi newtonienne de la gravitation universelle. Elle est l'expression d'un phénomène d'attraction; l'attraction est l'aiguillon du désir et le désir est l'essence de l'amour. Ainsi Eros n'est pas seulement maître des hommes et des dieux, mais l'animateur de la nature entière" (in *Poèsies complètes*, p. 723).

This organic philosophy is of course a romantic philosophy. For Musset, as for Fichte, motion is instinct; the stars and planets of his cosmos attract each other, not so much through gravitational pull as through desire; they organically strive toward each other just as Fichte's rivers "strive" toward the sea.[2]

But this universal attraction, this cosmic yearning, like Schopenhauer's Will, is never satisfied; never is anything or anyone at rest. Musset's vision is that of "une création toujours naissante et toujours moribonde," always in the throes of a feverish cyclical movement.

La terre se meurt; Herchele dit que c'est de froid. . . Cette grande loi d'attraction qui suspend le monde à sa place l'*use et le ronge* dans un désir sans fin; chaque planète *charrie* ses misères en gémissant sur son essieu; elles s'appellent d'un bout du ciel à l'autre, et inquiètes du repos, cherchent qui s'arrêtera la première. Dieu les retient; elles accomplissent assidument et éternellement leur labeur vide et inutile; elles *tournent*, elles souffrent, elles *brûlent*, elles *s'éteignent* et *s'allument*, elles *descendent* et *remontent*, elles *se suivent* et *s'évitent*, elles *s'enlacent* comme des anneaux; elles portent à leur surface des milliers d'êtres renouvelés sans cesse; ces êtres *s'agitent*, *se croisent* aussi, *se serrent* une heure les uns contre les autres, puis *tombent* et d'autres *se lèvent*. (*La Confession*; emphasis added)

The predominance here of verbs of motion is inevitable. Musset's world is that of Heraclitus and Democritus, a world of Whirl and Swirl. It is one in which one never steps into the same river twice; a world in which polite society is but a collection of "disconnected whirlwinds" (the image is used both in *La Confession* and *Les Caprices*) and deviations from it such as debauchery become tightrope walking and vertigo; a cosmos whose very planets are at the mercy not of mechanical but of emotional laws, unstable and unpredictable, of attraction and repulsion. In this vertiginous world man gropes desperately for permanent love and happiness, but in the end he gropes for straws.

PART TWO
Four Studies in Style and Genre

chapter five
MUSSET'S FIRST SONNET

Que j'aime le premier frisson d'hiver! le chaume
Sous le pied du chasseur, refusant de ployer!
Quand vient la pie aux champs que le foin vert embaume,
Au fond du vieux château s'éveille le foyer;

C'est le temps de la ville. —Oh! lorsque l'an dernier,
J'y revins, que je vis de son Louvre et son dôme,
Paris et sa fumée, et tout ce beau royaume
(J'entends encore au vent les postillons crier),

Que j'aimais ce temps gris, ces passants, et la Seine
Sous ses mille falots assise en souveraine!
J'allais revoir l'hiver. — Et toi, ma vie, et toi!

Oh! dans tes longs regards j'allais tremper mon âme;
Je saluais tes murs. — Car, qui m'eût dit, madame,
Que votre coeur sitôt avait changé pour moi?[1]

Musset is the only major French romantic to practice the sonnet. Sainte-Beuve also tried his hand at it but without success. Musset's sonnets have been praised for their deft handling of versification, but they should also be praised for their subtle handling of imagery as can be demonstrated by his first published sonnet. Thus far the poem has been analyzed in detail only once, in an unpublished doctoral dissertation. Fortunately the analysis is a good one. Here is a pertinent passage:

> The poem simultaneously celebrates a change of season and a change of heart... The "frisson" of the opening line establishes both the temporal and emotional climate of the poem, the poet's shiver at the first chill of winter, the shiver of anticipation as he returns to his mistress, and the ultimate chill of her rejection. Illuminated by the unexpected ending, the sonnet takes on a whole new dimension, and the reader is virtually sent back to the beginning again; it is almost circular in form, everything hinging on the *pointe* of his mistress' change of heart. The innocent pastoral imagery of the first quatrain, which seemed almost gratuitous on first reading, becomes more than a mere pictorial contrast with smoky Paris; the *chasseur* becomes the boy in search of love; the ground which refuses to yield, his mistress' hardened heart. . . .
>
> Images of inconstancy— *le vent, passants*, the flowing Seine, the momentary flickering of a thousand torches—combine to threaten any possibility of permanence.
>
> (James Hewitt, "Tropes of Self," pp. 161-62)

If one performs a semiotic operation on the sonnet, one can appreciate more fully the subtlety of this imagery of inconstancy and the unified or at least coherent thematic structure.[2]

One must take as the poem's invariant "deep structure" or matrix the narrator's ambivalence toward the sudden change in his relationship with this particular woman and in a broader and more significant sense his ambivalence toward change in general. Each variant will foreground either the positive or negative pole of the ambivalence. The negative pole (i.e., the lover's dismay) is explicit only at the end, in the surprising *pointe*.

> Car, qui m'eût dit, madame,
> Que votre coeur sitôt avait changé pour moi?
> (13-14)

The sudden twist, and the equally sudden grammatical change from the familiar to the polite, register the lover's shock. But the casual *qui m'eût dit* and the cool *madame* and *votre* that so quickly replace the tender (and repeated) *tes* and *toi* suggest that the narrator is far from crushed by this sudden change in his amorous fortunes. One can easily imagine him as a lover familiar with evanescent love affairs, as one, even, who rather enjoys a change of mistress from time to time. Although he is the unlucky victim this time, it is he, no doubt, whose heart first "changed" in some of his previous liaisons. This, surely, is not his first affair. If it were, the poem's tonality would be quite different.

Curiously, it is the positive side of the ambivalence (a lack of dismay and an enjoyment of change for its own sake) that the poem stresses, but in subtle ways.

> Que j'aime le premier frisson d'hiver!
> (1)
> Que j'aimais ce temps gris. . .
> (9)

This, in part, is sly preparation for the surprise ending, but the narrator's enthusiasm is genuine and is already ambivalent: it is inspired only secondarily by the lover's eager anticipation of the winter reunion with his mistress and primarily by the change of season and, by implication, Change in general.

The ambivalence is also reflected in the two colors used. The grey of winter (and of the smoky "city," which competes with the *champs* and the country *château*—still another ambivalent note) has not killed the green of the sweet-smelling hay. Here the narrator celebrates the continuity, the permanence of Nature's springtime color *in spite of* the change of season. In another but here sexual connotation, *vert* reinforces the fact that the lover's absence (*j'y revins*) has not diminished his ardor. This connotation, favorable to the mistress, will be challenged, however, by others.

The city is the object not only of the ambivalence mentioned above but of an ironic tension between the terms "beau royaume" and "fumée" and the almost mock-noble expression

La Seine
Sous ses milles falots assise en souveraine.
(9-10)

Pierre Citron (*Poésie de Paris*, p. 422) writes of this passage:

> On serait tenté aujourd'hui de voir dans la juxtaposition des falots et de la souveraine quelque ironie volontaire à l'égard de la solennité de l'expression; mais ce serait sans doute être trop subtil, d'autant plus que les mots "la Seine souveraine" se retrouvent bien plus tard, chez Sainte-Beuve, dans un poème où il n'est pas question de chercher de l'ironie (*Livre d'amour*). Car, pour la plupart des romantiques, la Seine reste un des éléments les plus nobles de Paris.

This is a just appraisal. There is no sarcastic irony here but ambivalence, what Citron calls "admiration désinvolte" (p. 213) for Paris.

Images of inconstancy, impermanence and change are coextensive with the text; they provide its formal constant. It is well known now that such equivalences (Jakobson) or parallelisms (Nicolas Ruwet) are the very stuff of the poetic function.[3] They create what Michael Riffaterre calls overdetermination, which is denser in poetry than in the other literary genres. To the four images listed by James Hewitt—the wind, the passers-by, the flowing river, the flickering torches—should be added seven others: the *premier frisson d'hiver* (three of the four words are operative here); the *chaume* (The withered stalks of the first line offer an implicit analogy with the dried-up heart of the last line, just as the first chill of winter parallels the final "chill of her rejection;" the smoke in line 7; the impatient *postillons* who shout at the wind in line 8; and, most interesting, the bird in movement of line 3.

The choice of bird, the unprepossessing magpie, is a surprising one in a love poem and in the idyllic "pastoral" scene the poet sets in the first quatrain. That is, it contrasts with the microcontext and creates a stylistic effect which must be accounted for. In the stereotypes associated with the word *pie* (the word's "descriptive system," to use Riffaterre's terminology) there are no positive connotations such as avian beauty of color or song. The magpie has an ungainly long tail and is noted for its chattering call, its shrill piping. It is a pest, a scavenger, attracted to bright, gaudy objects and addicted to stealing them for its nest. In the clichés labeled upon male victims it is the bird's thievous nature that is consecrated: *larron comme une pie.* The stereotype has served as title to an opera, Rossini's *La Gazza Ladra,* whose libretto is taken from a French melodrama, *La Pie voleuse.* (The basic structural principle of melodrama is, of course, the stereotype.) The opera was to become one of Musset's favorites, the leading role being sung in his day by none other than La Malibran. Like the magpie, our poet-lover has thievously stolen the love of a married ("madame") lady, who no doubt wears the bright, sometimes gaudy and often overdressed attire of the nobility. The clichés derived from *pie* that are attached to female victims also deflate indirectly (poetry *is* indirection) the poem's heroine: *jaser comme une pie; jacasser comme une pie; une femme bavarde comme une pie; comme une pie borgne; c'est une vraie pie*—expressions that work subliminally on the reader to suggest the frivolousness of the poet's ex-mistress and by logical extension the frivolousness of the French aristocracy, which *de* Musset knew so well: he was a card-carrying member, in fact rather inordinately proud, his biographers tell us, of his *carte de visite.* But the young aristocrat's natural shyness often deflated his vanity: Lamartine has spoken of Musset's "silence modeste et habituel au milieu du tumulte confus d'une société *jaseuse* de femmes et de poètes" (quoted by Arvède Barine, *Musset,* p. 34). A more explicit sign of frivolousness is the fickleness clearly suggested at the end: "sitôt avait changé"—*sitôt* is given special emphasis by being removed from its usual syntactic slot. Musset frequented both aristocratic ladies and common whores but addressed poems and the polite "vous, madame," only to the former. One biographer has guessed that the real-life heroine of this poem is an aristocratic lady from Saint-Denis who refused to take Musset's eighteen years seriously.

For the poem's reader the impact of all these stereotypes in the magpie "mythology" is to *suggest* (poetry *is* suggestiveness) the poet's ambivalence toward his mistress and thus his misfortune. (Gogol has used the same mythology to introduce a dissonant note: A magpie appears in *The Inspector General* just as the false inspector steals a kiss from the mayor's wife.) To proclaim rather than suggest his ambivalence would be tantamount to deflating prosaically, and in public, the mistress' rating on a scale of one to ten and thus the lover's taste in women. His ambivalence is reinforced by the fact that he will probably (being a *chasseur*—a contemporary poet might have used *dragueur*) find an adequate replacement for her. It is even reflected in the predominant color, grey, which depicts not just the seasonal but what Hewitt calls the poem's emotional climate.

To put the matter differently: One of the significate effects (Pierce) of the sign-vehicle *pie* is a warning signal that serves as preparation, even adumbration, for the sudden change of direction the poem will take at the end, thus giving it a tighter thematic structure than an initial reading would suggest. Another significate effect of the word is to temper the narrator's delight at the beginning and his dismay at the end. The word's location, its great distance from the *madame* at the end of the poem, should not deceive us: Semiotic displacement behaves much like that produced in neurosis: the repressing of censored material from the matrix (here, the lover's ambivalence) produces symptoms in other parts than the affected one, and the transmission of the patient's (i.e., sufferer's) real message becomes scrambled.[4]

The surprise ending does force the reader to return to the beginning or at least read retroactively. The *chasseur* then becomes a lover in the Don Juan mould, the *frisson* becomes the "thrill of the chase," the hard ground refusing to yield is Don Juan's challenge, the winning of a woman who once played "hard to get" and who now is hard to keep. It has been a year (*l'an dernier*) since she has been out from under his foot (*sous le pied du chasseur*). But the poem itself is testimony to the fact that the rejected lover is keeping open the lines of communication in an ambivalent or lukewarm *(qui m'eût dit; pie; votre)* attempt to win her back.

What is impressive in the sonnet is the subtle and unobtrusive way the imagery reflects not only the ambivalent mood of the narrator but the mobility and changeability of his world. Never do the objects become hardened into objective correlatives (one hesitates even to speak of symbols) or softened into the pathetic fallacy. Unobtrusive as they are, they are there in very significant number and *converge* to turn surface significance into *signifiance* and point to a world of radical impermanence.

*
* *

I have read "into" the poem because that is what readers are supposed to do. The very *non-dit* of the sonnet is an invitation to reader participation. Here is the pre-Symbolist Musset himself on the subject of poetic indirection, suggestiveness and the *non-dit*: "Dans tout vers remarquable d'un vrai poète, il y a deux ou trois fois plus que ce qui est dit; c'est au lecteur à suppléer le reste, selon ses idées, sa force, ses goûts" (*OEuvres complètes*, p. 650) The ambivalence I find is justified by the poem's subtle and polyvalent tonality and also by the intertextual impact of the poet's entire opus: If a literary text is a mosaic of quotations (Barthes and Kristeva), the most significant quotations are those in which the poet quotes himself. This early poem will have many echoes in Musset's subsequent work and it is itself an echo of earlier and contemporary pieces. The sonnet did not appear in a vacuum but in Musset's first published volume, the *Contes d'Espagne et d'Italie*, which contains long tales of sexual infidelity and shorter pieces, like our sonnet, that sing of superficial love.

> Or si d'aventure on s'enquête
> Qui m'a valu telle conquête,
> C'est l'allure de mon cheval,
> Un compliment sur sa mantille,
> Puis des bonbons à la vanille. . . .
> ("Madrid")

The inevitability of change and impermanence, as demonstrated in the previous chapter, is Musset's major theme. His own ambivalence toward change, especially in matters of love, can easily be documented. I appeal here not to biography, which is convincingly corroborative, but to the personae of his poems. While it is true that the personae of a romantic poet are by definition autobiographical, the fact is of interest only to biographers. Musset's *summum bonum* is love. But love, like all human sentiments, is subject to what he considers Nature's two basic laws: change and entropy: "Tout s'en va;" "Tout s'évanouit;" "Tout meurt;" "Tout s'use." While Musset bemoans the inevitability of change, inconstancy and impermanence in his elegiac lyrics, his cynical Don Juans—Rafaël, Mardoche, Hassan—revel in their constant change of mistresses. To love they say, is the main thing, what matters the mistress? What matters the bottle if it brings intoxication? What Musset said of himself can be said of them: They can fall in love as easily as they catch a cold. For Rafaël a love affair that lasts two years is already "a bit long." For Mardoche six months are more than enough to "changer d'amour." Hassan's limit is a week! For all of them it is the thrill of the chase, the winning of an unwilling maiden, that is love's chief challenge and charm, but—

Mais, dès qu'elle se rend, bonsoir, le charme cesse.

. . .

L'amour (hélas! l'étrange et la fausse nature!)
Vit d'inanition et meurt de nourriture.

(Mardoche)

The mistress' change of heart at the end of our sonnet is regretted but surely forgiven. In a poem written just a year later the lover will switch roles with the sonnet's fickle mistress.

J'ai dit à mon coeur, à mon pauvre coeur:
N'est-ce pas assez d'aimer sa maîtresse?
Et ne vois-tu pas que *changer* sans cesse,
C'est perdre en désirs le temps du bonheur?

Il m'a répondu: Ce n'est point assez.
Ce n'est point assez d'aimer sa maîtresse!
Et ne vois-tu pas que *changer* sans cesse
Nous rend doux et chers les plaisirs passés?

("Chanson;" our emphasis)

George Sand attributes to the Musset of *Elle et Lui* (Laurent) the idea that the pleasure of change is perhaps the whole secret of life and that to change is to renew oneself. And in "A la Mi-Carême" the poet says that "notre esprit inconstant. . . vit de changement." The poet's ambivalence toward change in the poem above is expressed directly by the *dédoublement*, the *je/ coeur* antithesis. This ambivalent *dédoublement* will become one of Musset's recurrent motifs, the most famous example being the Octave/ Coelio duo of *Les Caprices de Marianne.*

In a more serious vein Musset developed a third law of love, the law of perpetual renewal (i.e., conservation of emotional energy). Individual love affairs are ephemeral, but Love itself is eternal.

Quand j'ai passé par la prairie,
J'ai vu, ce soir, dans le sentier,
Une fleur tremblante et flétrie,
Une pâle fleur d'églantier.
Un bourgeon vert à côté d'elle
Se balançait sur l'arbrisseau!
Je vis poindre une fleur nouvelle;
La plus jeune était la plus belle:
L'homme est ainsi, toujours nouveau.

. . .

Puisque tout meurt ce soir pour revivre demain. . .

. . .

Il faut aimer sans cesse, après avoir aimé.

(La Nuit d'Août)

While he here proclaims love as a perpetual continuum, the actual partners involved are constantly changing in this hectic cyclical movement or treadmill. Here too one senses ambivalence. Musset's theory of perpetual love is proclaimed triumphantly (the *puisque* being repeated anaphorically a half-dozen times), but in the context of his entire opus, more especially in the *Nuit* cycle, the theory seems to be, in part, a *pis-aller*, a frantic effort to believe in love despite its frustratingly transient nature. Again, what is impressive in the sonnet is that so much of all this is suggested in the short space of fourteen lines. To the virtue mentioned earlier, its subtlety, should be added its density, its suggestiveness and multiple associations, which make re-readings of the poem rewarding.

chapter six
ROMANTIC IRONY IN MUSSET'S
NAMOUNA

Since romantic irony, as Henri Peyre has pointed out, has been studied chiefly by German scholars, and since the German scholars themselves have been in rather radical disagreement as to the precise nature of this form of irony, a working definition may be in order at the outset.[1] In *A Dictionary of Literary Terms* we are told that "The romantic ironist detaches himself from his own artistic creation, treating it playfully or objectively, thus presumably showing his complete freedom."[2] Henri Peyre stresses the crucial point that this ironic detachment comes not after but during the creative performance itself: "Through that irony, the creator stressed his indepence of his own creation precisely as he was accomplishing it" (p. 141). It should also be stressed that the ironic detachment, playfulness, self-parody and so forth, is imposed upon a material that is fundamentally, or at least in large measure, *serious*— hence the irony. We are dealing, then, with a rather complex and highly paradoxical form of irony. The author presents us with a theme or a hero that he takes seriously to a significant degree, but he nonetheless cannot take his work as a whole with total seriousness nor can he relate to his hero with total sympathy.

There may very well be as many reasons for an author to have recourse to romantic irony as there are authors. For Germans like Schlegel, romantic irony is an intangible spirit hovering over the whole work and reflects a metaphysical stance: "The universe as experienced by man is for Schlegel an infinitude which cannot be reduced to rational order, a chaos, a complex of contradiction and incongruity, for our limited intellects cannot fathom the order of the absolute. We may at times catch a glimpse of this order, but once we try to realize it for ourselves or express it to others we are involved in contradiction or paradox."[3] For English and French writers, especially Byron, Musset and Stendhal, romantic irony is a less transcendental and more tangible phenomenon and is readily identifiable by the specific stylistic devices and literary strategies employed.

One impetus to romantic irony was the desire to avoid the embarrassing sentimentality, bathos and hyperbole that marred so much preromantic literature. One antidote administered by the romantic ironist is the sudden passage from one mood to another, for example having hot baths of sentiment followed by cold douches of irony, as Jean-Paul Richter put it. Another is to break the spell of poetic enthusiasm or exalted sentiment by a cumbersome intrusion of the author's presence (subjective irony). Or the hero can be placed in an embarrassing or demeaning situation (objective irony). Or the author can apologize to the reader for the weakness of the poem or novel in progress (naive irony). A well known example of romantic irony is the passage in Byron's *Don Juan* in which the hero indulges in blatant hyperbole and sentimentality when taking leave of his mistress and Spain, then suddenly, and anticlimactically, becomes sea-sick.

> And oh! if e'er I should forget, I swear—
> But that's impossible, and cannot be—
> Sooner shall this blue Ocean melt to air,
> Sooner shall Earth resolve itself to sea,
> Than I resign thine image, oh, my fair!
> Or think of anything, excepting thee;
> A mind diseased no remedy can physic—
> (Here the ship gave a lurch, and he grew sea-sick.)
>
> Sooner shall Heaven kiss earth—here he fell sicker)
> Oh, Julia! What is every other woe? —
> (For God's sake let me have a glass of liquor;
> Pedro, Battista, help me down below.)
> Julia, my love — (you rascal, Pedro, quicker)—
> Oh, Julia— (this curst vessel pitches so)—
> Belovèd Julia, hear me still beseeching!
> (Here he grew inarticulate with retching.)

A second impetus to romantic irony was the tendency of the romantic imagination to view History as a mixture of grandeur and farce or, as Edmund Burke expressed it, a "monstrous tragi-comic scene."[4] This view of History precludes on the author's part an attitude of total seriousness toward what he is trying to accomplish. A third impetus arose from the fact that the romantic age was, among many other things, an age of irony: "Le sentiment est mort, l'esprit sec: on tourne en plaisanterie les choses les plus respectables et qui furent, jadis, respectées" (V. Brunet, *Lyrisme de Musset*, p. 349). A fourth source of romantic irony was the tension between the romantic author's search for the Ideal and the *simultaneous* awareness of the search's futility. Paul Bourget has spoken of Heine and Musset as iconoclasts adoring the idols they break.

> Qu'ils s'en rendent compte ou non, ils sont, comme nous tous, les produits d'une époque de critique inexorable, de réflexion méthodique, d'analyse acharnée et méticuleuse, de

Science, enfin. "Anatomistes et physiologistes," s'écriait Sainte-Beuve après *Madame Bovary*, "je vous retrouve partout!"
. . . . qui fait inévitablement d'un homme un iconoclaste intellectuel. Que cet iconoclaste ait gardé en même temps les naïves ferveurs de la foi, qu'il ne puisse se retenir d'adorer l'idole en la brisant, d'aimer avec frénésie ce qu'il dissèque avec férocité, que toutes les exaltations du désir et de la tendresse s'unissent en lui à toutes les lucidités du désenchantement—quelle misère! Quelle anomalie! C'est le lot quotidien de l'homme moderne, cependant, et ce fut la destinée de Musset, aussi bien que de Heine. (*Sociologie et Littérature* p. 267).

A fifth source was the tendency, related to that of the ambivalent iconoclast, to institute a critical self-analysis at the very moment an emotion or a dramatic action reached its peak of intensity.

Je place Scribe très haut, said Musset in a conversation reported by M. Legouvé, mais il a un défaut, *il ne se fâche jamais contre lui-même*. —Que voulez-vous dire par là?—Je veux dire que quand Scribe commence une pièce, un acte, ou une scène, il suit toujours d'où il part, par où il passe, et où il arrive. De là sans doute *un mérite de ligne droite*, qui donne grande solidité à ce qu'il écrit. Il est trop logique; il ne perd jamais la tête. Moi, au contraire, au courant d'une scène ou d'un morceau de poésie, il m'arrive tout à coup de changer de route, de culbuter mon propre plan, de me retourner contre mon personnage préféré, et de le faire battre par son interlocuteur. . . J'étais parti pour Madrid et je vais à Constantinople. (Quoted by Léon Séché, *Musset*, I, p. 109)

A sixth source was an instinctive defense mechanism that prompted writers like Musset to hide and protect their *vrai moi* under a paradoxical kaleidoscope of masks.

Loin de s'offrir directement au public, loin de chanter ses amours, sa foi politique, sa religion, sa place dans la société, Musset ne se met en scène que par plaisanterie, et s'il dessine son portrait, c'est en caricaturiste; il ne veut livrer de lui-même qu'une image amusante et contradictoire qui lui permette d'échapper à l'emprise des lecteurs et de sauvegarder l'intégrité foncière de son coeur.
(P. Van Tieghem, *Musset*, p. 21)

En effet, il présente ainsi à ses semblables plusieurs personnages successifs et contingents dont chacun suggère un monde en fait inexistant, trompant ainsi les autres et les empêchant de deviner l'être profond et de l'attaquer.
(C. Dolder, *L'Etre et le paraître*, p. 39)

A seventh impetus was the modern tendency to see man not as the classical *homme absolu* but as a paradoxical animal who can be depicted accurately only in terms of paradox. Man, according to this view, is a complex network of contradictory impulses, wavering between idealism and cynicism, between altruism and solipsism, between reason and emotion and, for the orthodox, between good and evil.

Historically, it was Victor Hugo who first asked his fellow romantics in France to ponder the aesthetic implications of man's dualism. One can therefore take 1827 and the *Préface de Cromwell*, not as the actual starting point (for reasons that will be discussed immediately), but as the initial springboard or "call for" romantic irony in France. It is Alfred de Musset who is its first real practitioner in poetry and in drama.

In his influential Preface, Hugo argues for a Shakespearean mixture of the comic and tragic because such a mixture is found in the very heart and soul of man and therefore at the very center of the human experience. Robert Penn Warren, explaining the importance of the coarse humor of Mercutio in *Romeo and Juliet*, says that "the poet wishes to indicate that his vision has been earned, that it can survive reference to the complexities and contradictions of experience ("Impure Poetry," p. 252). But Shakespeare's vision is "earned" not simply through this rather facile structural device but chiefly through the density of his characterization and style. Hugo, rather naively, thought that the mere juxtaposition of the comic and tragic, the sublime and the grotesque, would guarantee that the romantic drama would achieve this earned vision and that it would capture life in its very complexity. But Hugo's *mélange des genres* is mere antithesis, not ambivalence or paradox. There is no romantic irony to be found in the Hugolian Hero. He may rub elbows with buffoons in comic scenes tacked on to the main business at hand, but his attitude toward himself remains essentially simple: He takes himself seriously and even tragically. So does the author.

Alfred de Musset's heroes on the other hand often give off a sense of romantic irony not just because one can feel *within the same character* a tension between opposite impulses, but especially because the author's attitude toward his characters as well as their own attitude toward themselves seems ambivalent. Their cynical frivolousness is presented initially as the only appropriate life style in view of their *Weltschmerz*. But at the same time they do not take their cynicism too seriously. They tend to see themselves, rather, as sad clowns—a type of hero to which we have become accustomed in the twentieth century since it is one of the chief heroes of our literature and of our painting. Fantasio, for example, remains unemployed because, he says, people don't hire teachers of Melancholy; and so, to escape his creditors, he gaily dons the jester's togs. Octave, in *Les Caprices de Marianne*, another instructor in Melancholy, carries as his sword "une batte d'Arlequin." But just as we are getting used to interpreting Octave and Fantasio as silly, flippant clowns, they turn out to be, in their role as friends, both steadfast and courageous. One effect of romantic irony is immediately obvious: it tends to keep the reader either off balance or very much on his toes.

As Byron had done for English literature, Musset created a special breed of romantic hero: the cynical, playful débauché who does not take Life too seriously and who lives his own life, as Baudelaire will ironize a quarter-century later, "under the whip of Pleasure, that merciless torturer." One is tempted to call him the Ambivalent Hero, who does not simply laugh while crying, as Heine's heroes do, but who makes fun of his own distress or, when he makes fun of others, it is with a nuance of regret. In *La Coupe et les Lèvres* the Chorus asks Frank: "Te fais-tu le bouffon de ta propre détresse?" and a page later: "Tu railles tristement et misérablement."

This ironic tension between idealism and cynicism is found in *Namouna*, one of Musset's longest but least understood poems. What little attention has been given to the poem has been directed mainly at the Don Juan figure that the poet sketches in the second canto. Nowhere is there a discussion of the romantic irony that informs the poem from beginning to end and that provides the key to an understanding of the poem's total impact.[5]

*
* *

Irony in Musset is basically a tendency to deflate, often at the expense of his fellow romantics, often at his own expense. When the irony is directed at certain tendencies of the romantic movement, this, of course, is *not* romantic irony since the author is not identifying in the least with what he is mocking. For example, when Musset irreverently likens the moon shining over a belfrey to a trivial dot over an *i*, or a Byronic hero perched on the Jungfrau to a fly on a sugar loaf, he is not deflating his own style but the clichés of his contemporaries. Similarly, when Musset, in *Namouna* (I, 23-24)[6], apologizes for the lack of local color in this "oriental tale," because, he says, he has never been to the orient and has "never stolen anything from a library," this is not true romantic irony either since it is really directed at the superficial local color of Hugo's *Orientales*. In a passage such as the following, from the *dédicace* to *La Coupe et les Lèvres*—

> Vous me demanderez si j'aime ma patrie.
> Oui; —j'aime fort aussi l'Espagne et la Turquie.
>
> . . .
>
> Vous me demanderez si je suis catholique.
> Oui; —j'aime aussi les dieux Lath et Nésu.
>
> . . .
>
> Vous me demanderez si j'aime la sagesse.
> Oui; —j'aime fort aussi le tabac à fumer.

—the last line, on first reading, may seem to be deflating the author's own ego, but the context and the parallel structure of the couplets make it clear that the irony is still being directed outward at conventional wisdom, just as it is against patriotism and catholicism, rather than the author's supposed hedonism and anti-intellectualism. It is conventional life, not the poet himself that is not being taken seriously, just as in Byron's lines—

> I say—the future is a serious matter—
> And so—for God's sake—hock and soda water.[7]

However, in *Namouna* we witness a curious mixture of irony-at-the-expense-of-romanticism and romantic irony, the latter directed against Hassan, the very hero of Musset's poem. Consider the following passage:

> Il n'avait ni parents, ni guenon, ni maîtresse.
> Rien d'ordinaire en lui, —rien qui le rattachât
> Au commun des martyrs, — pas un chien, pas un chat.
> Il faut cependant bien que je vous intéresse
> A mon pauvre héros. — Dire qu'il est pacha,
> C'est un moyen usé, c'est une maladresse.
> Dire qu'il est grognon, sombre et mystérieux,
> Ce n'est pas vrai d'abord, et c'est encor plus vieux.
> (I, 27-28)

Musset is poking fun at the hackneyed hero of romanticism: the orphan, the outcast, the pariah, solitary both in his *état civil* and in his moral-intellectual superiority, the *beau ténébreux*: somber, mysterious, misanthropic and melancholy. But at the same time he is deflating his own hero. First, he dashes the reader's hopes of encountering a more flamboyant hero and, more importantly, he abruptly halts the narrative to ponder the technical problem of enlisting the reader's sympathy. Throughout the entire poem, as here, the narration of Hassan's story is interrupted thematically by the intrusions of the author and structurally by the intrusion of the present tense upon the regular narrative tenses. The reader is constantly shuttled between the past exploits of Hassan and the present preoccupations of his creator.

The intrusion of the present tense begins as early as the poem's second stanza:

> Hassan avait d'ailleurs une très noble pose,
> Il était nu comme Eve à son premier péché.
> Quoi! tout nu! n'avait-il pas de honte?
> Nu, dès le second mot! —Que sera-ce à la fin?
> Monsieur, excusez-moi, —je commence ce conte
> Juste quand mon héros vient de sortir du bain.
>
> (I, 1-2)

The description of Hassan's *entrée en scène*—deflating in itself—is interrupted first by the anticipated exclamations of the scandalized reader and later by the vocative and imperative of the penultimate line. Then the narrative completely breaks down as Musset switches to the present of the narrative act: "Je commence ce conte/Juste quand. . . ."

Musset constantly uses the present tense to express his independence of his hero:

> Au fait, s'il agit mal, on pourrait rêver pire. —
> Ma foi, tant pis pour lui: —je ne vois pas pourquoi
> Les sottises d'Hassan retomberaient sur moi.
>
> (I, 30)

> —Je rappelle au lecteur qu'ici comme là-bas
> C'est mon héros qui parle, et je mourrais de honte
> S'il croyait un instant que ce que je raconte
> Ici plus que jamais, ne me révolte pas.
>
> (I, 39)

In his brilliant analysis of a passage form Rousseau's *Confessions* Jean Starobinski (*L'Oeil vivant*, II, p. 115) has shown how the author achieves subtle ironic effects by shifting from the narrative past to the present as "qualitatively privileged tense," or what other critics have called "the ethical present." The present of the narrative act conveys not only a foreknowledge of what is going to be related (and is thus invested with Sophoclean irony) but also the superior wisdom and experience of the writer writing *now*, so that the relation of author to character (or, in Rousseau's case, of author-past vs. author-present) is one of amused condescension. We are dealing with romantic irony here because Musset, like Rousseau, does identify with the character he is mocking. It must be borne in mind that romantic irony is a double irony, it works in two opposite directions at once: the poet will declare himself alienated from his hero, but this alienation itself is also ironic—it masks the author's limited but genuinely sympathetic identification. Despite his many (ironic) declarations of independence and detachment, Musset offers Hassan, as we shall see, as an important incarnation of his world view. The role of Hassan, no less than that of Rolla, Octave, Fantasio, Frank or Lorenzaccio, has serious implications that have been consistently overlooked by the critics.

By stanza 32 the romantic irony shifts from the hero to the poet himself who despairs of being able to finish his rambling poem; that is, there is a shift from subjective and objective irony to naive irony. In stanza 61 Musset admits having disgressed so long that he has forgotten where he has left his story. Then he will apologize to the reader for a hiatus here, a barbarism there, and so forth. What we really have here is romantic irony in triplicate: first, the poet pokes fun at his hero; then at himself and his poem; and finally the reader is constantly discouraged from identifying with Hassan by being made self-conscious through the many vocatives directed at him by the poet. The hero is constantly wedged between the reader and the writer:

> Tu vois, lecteur, jusqu'où va ma franchise,
> Mon héros est tout nu, —moi je suis en chemise.
> (I, 75)

Another source of romantic irony in *Namouna* is the poem's overall structure. Musset keeps promising his reader to get on with the story but keeps putting it off. The narrative proper does not begin until the third and final canto—a mere fourteen stanzas compared to the fifty-five stanzas of the second canto and the seventy-eight stanzas of the first. The poet even devotes the first four of the final fourteen stanzas to still another apology for rambling off the subject, leaving only the last sixty lines (out of a total of 882) to the actual plot of this "oriental tale." Thus the hero of the story and the story itself are treated with ironic detachment and are deconstructed from beginning to end.[8] The obvious fact is that we are not dealing with narrative poetry at all—even to mock the heroic would require more narrative than we are given—but with the poetry of ideas. The poem must be read not only on its comic level (brilliantly done in itself) but on a deeper one.

*

* *

The second canto is a digression (i.e., another instance of structural irony) and is devoted, not to Hassan at all, but to Musset's idea of the perfect Don Juan. Musset's Don Juan has none of the vulgarity, the gratuitous cruelty, the hatred of both God and man found in many of his illustrious predecessors:

> C'est qu'avec leurs horreurs, leur doute et leur blasphème
> Pas un ne t'aimait, Don Juan; et moi, je t'aime.
> (II, 39)

He is rather the "candide corrupteur," loving and leaving three thousand women in his search for the ideal one. It is important to note that the hyperbolic figure, tripling the usual number of Don Juan's conquests is serious rather than comic in effect. Although his thirst—which is of a moral and aesthetic as well as erotic nature—is never satisfactorily quenched, Don Juan never gives up hope:

> . . . tu mourus plein d'espoir.
> Tu perdis ta beauté, ta gloire et ton génie
> Pour un être impossible et qui n'existait pas.
> (II, 53)

There is no sadism in Don Juan's dealings with women, only a fierce optimism urging him on in his quest.

The relationship between this idealized Don Juan and Hassan is crucial for an appreciation of the total impact of the poem. The relationship is expressed in the last two lines of the canto:

> Ce que don Juan aimait, Hassan l'aimait peut-être.
> Ce que don Juan cherchait, Hassan n'y croyait pas.

Thus Don Juan goes from woman to woman because of an impossible dream, a quixotic quest, whereas Hassan goes from woman to woman since, knowing such a quest is hopeless, one woman is as good as another.[9] Although Musset is stressing the difference between the two types of Don Juan in the lines quoted above, they are nevertheless linked not only by the parallel syntax but also by the tentative "peut-être," suggesting a latent idealism in Hassan: he would gladly remain faithful to a perfect woman if such a woman existed. Hassan's doubt links him to the author ("un être impossible et qui n'existait pas"). In fact there can be no doubt that Hassan, no less than Musset's other heroes, is a projection of the poet himself, a point that is important to keep in mind when judging the causes and effects of romantic irony.

On its deepest level the poem, despite its comic surface, must be read as a somber meditation on the ethical implications of a world devoid of a perfect being in heaven as well as on earth and denied self-delusion by virtue of its new-found skepticism. The only response to such a bleak situation is Hassan's quantitative ethic: since the spiritual longings of man will never be satisfied, the modern Don Juan (Hassan) must live within the confines of the senses, deriving what consolation from them he can and prolonging his transient pleasures as long as he can.

One of the curious effects of the second canto is that, while Hassan does not even figure in it, sympathy is indirectly built up for him. We have mentioned the latent idealism: it is only Hassan's superior lucidity (Voltaire's men have by now been born) that prevents him from being as naively idealistic as Don Juan. There is also the suggestion of a certain courage, for Hassan as well as for Don Juan, to live in the face of ugly Reality. And the absense of self-pity, automatically precluded by the romantic irony, makes Hassan more sympathetic than many another romantic hero.

But the romantic irony also prevents Hassan from being inflated into an idealized creation. The chief source of irony directed against him is the fact that he is not only obliged to compete with but is overshadowed by the Don Juan of the canto-long digression. But Don Juan, too, is a victim of romantic irony: he is treated seriously but is wedged between the Hassan of the first and final cantos which are, furthermore, written basically in a comic vein. The final irony is that neither hero is given the total role, which belongs to an inconsequential servant girl whose plight is described in less than thirty lines. The total effect of the poem—and this seems to have escaped all the critics—is an irony directed at modern man: with our disabused cynicism and scientism, our unredeemed sensualism, Hassan is the only Don Juan figure we deserve.

*
* *

There is a significant passage at the beginning of *Namouna* that throws light not only of the poem itself but also on the particular kind of vision that impels that poet to use it.

Vous souvient-il,lecteur, de cette sérénade
Que don Juan, déguisé, chante sous un balcon?
—Une mélancolique et piteuse chanson,
Respirant la douleur, l'amour et la tristesse.

Mais l'accompagnement parle d'un autre ton.
Comme il est vif, joyeux! avec quelle prestesse
Il sautille!—On dirait que la chanson caresse

Et couvre de langueur le perfide instrument,
Tandis que l'air moqueur de l'accompagnement
Tourne en dérision la chanson elle-même,
Et semble railler d'aller si tristement.
Tout cela cependant fait un plaisir extrême.
(I, 13-14)

This "extreme" aesthetic pleasure, produced by the ironic counterpoint in *Don Giovanni* is based on the spectator's recognition of a psychological and moral truth:

C'est que tout en est vrai, —c'est qu'on trompe et qu'on aime;
C'est qu'on pleure en riant; — c'est qu'on est innocent
Et coupable à la fois; — c'est qu'on se croit parjure
Lorsqu'on n'est qu'abusé; c'est qu'on verse le sang
Avec des mains sans tache, et que notre nature
A de mal et de bien pétri sa créature:
Tel est le monde, hélas! et tel était Hassan.
(I, 15-16)

Thus, just as convincingly and much more succinctly than the *Préface de Cromwell*, this mini-manifesto urges a *mélange des genres* based on a view of man not as a smooth monolith but as a creature of ambivalence and paradox, what Laforgue will call "l'innombrable clavier humain." Musset's description of Hassan, which immediately precedes this passage, provides an illustration:

Il était très joyeux, et pourtant très maussade.
Détestable voisin, —excellent camarade,
Extrêmement futil, —et pourtant très posé,
Indignement naïf, —et pourtant très blasé,
Horriblement sincère, —et pourtant très rusé.
(I, 13)

Romantic irony is more than a stylistic device used in the service of a limited context: it is a mode of vision with psychological and philosophical implications. The author's ambivalent attitude (alienation—identification; antipathy—sympathy) toward the hero of his story stems from a moral agnosticism informed by a view of the human psyche as fundamentally unstable, contradictory and unpredictable, or, as Montaigne and Gide would put it, *ondoyant et divers*. The pseudo-scientific foresight of an earlier generation of *idéologues* and, for that matter, the more modest hindsight of our own generation's *caractérologues*, are summarily dismissed by a skeptical irony directed not only outward at the incomprehensible Other but also at the elusive, slippery Self. This instability, this multiple ego or, if you prefer, this existential freedom, will be studied extensively in the twentieth century by writers as different as Proust, Pirandello, Eugene O'Neill and Nathalie Sarraute. Romantic irony is based on the ambiguity of feelings ("La gaieté est quelquefois triste, et la mélancolie a le sourire sur les lèvres" [*André Del Sarto*]), the ambiguity of knowledge ("ce que vous dites là est parfaitement juste, et parfaitement faux, comme tout au monde" [*Lorenzaccio*]), the ambiguity of morals ("ce mélange de fange et de ciel" [Letter to Paul Foucher], and the ambiguity and inadequacy of language ("Quelle parole humaine exprimera jamais la plus faible caresse" [*Confession d'un enfant du siècle*]; "Que les mots sont froids, insignifiants, que la parole est misérable quand on veut essayer de dire combien l'on aime!" [*Bettine*]).[10]

The originality of Musset's paradoxical vision in *Namouna*, especially within the historical context of the romantic movement, is pointed out by Philippe Van Tieghem: "Pour la première fois, Musset, dans ce poème, a trouvé son domaine propre: le point de jonction de l'idéal et de la corruption, du plaisir et du désespoir. Un pareil motif d'inspiration est plus dramatique que lyrique, parce que la position de l'auteur est éminemment instable et contradictoire; elle s'oppose à la position statique de l'idéalisme de Lamartine et au dynanisme optimiste de Hugo" (*Musset*, p. 47).

Thus nineteenth-century French literature is given a new kind of comic vision, tinged with sadness and seriousness, but not taking the seriousness too seriously. It started with Musset in poetry and in drama and with Stendhal in the novel and will have distinguished variations performed by Gautier, Flaubert, Charles Cros and Laforgue. The twentieth century will take romantic irony and turn it into *humour noir*: the playfulness will still be there, but the tragic overtones will be emphasized. With romantic irony we are still dealing with skepticism and disillusionment leading to a comic sense of life.

chapter seven
MUSSET'S *SOUVENIR* AND THE GREATER ROMANTIC LYRIC

The earliest formal invention produced by romantic poets is a genre that Meyer Abrams has called the "greater Romantic lyric," a genre that evolved out of eighteenth-century loco-descriptive poetry and that includes such well known poems as Coleridge's *The Eolian Harp* and *Fears in Solitude*, Wordsworth's *Tintern Abbey*, Shelley's *Stanzas Written in Dejection*, Keat's *Ode to a Nightingale* and Schiller's *Der Spaziergang*.[1] It is only recently that the genre has been shown to include French poems as well, specifically *Tristesse d'Olympio* and *Le Lac*.[2] That *Souvenir* is very similar thematically to *Le Lac* and to *Tristesse d'Olympio* is a cliché of literary history; that it is an important exemplar of the greater Romantic lyric is a fact that needs to be demonstrated. The purpose of this essay is to provide such a demonstration by placing Musset's poem in this larger generic context.

The greater Romantic lyric, as described by Abrams, is an extended poem involving a description of a natural setting, an interaction or interinvolvement between the setting and the observing subject modulating into a sustained meditation that interweaves perceptual, personal and philosophical elements and that produces thus a *paysage moralisé*. It presents a determinate speaker in a particularized setting, whom we overhear as he carries on a sustained colloquy either with himself, with the outer scene or with a silent human auditor, present or absent. It exhibits in particular two basic patterns of experience and formal thematic development with a third pattern often present:

> The speaker begins with a description of the landscape; an aspect or change of aspect in the landscape evokes a varied but integral process of memory, thought, anticipation, and feeling which remains closely interinvolved with the outer scene. In the course of this meditation the lyric speaker achieves an insight, faces up to a tragic loss, comes to a moral decision, or resolves the emotional problem. Often the poem rounds upon itself to end where it began, at the outer scene, but with an altered mood and deepened understanding, which is the result of the intervening meditation.
> ("Greater Romantic Lyric," pp. 527-28)

As Abrams asserts, this controlled and shapely lyric is of great interest not only because it was the first romantic formal invention, but also

because it was so very prevalent during the romantic period and because
it engendered so many successors. Variations on the genre were performed
by Matthew Arnold, Walt Whitman, William Butler Yeats and more
recently by Wallace Stevens and W. H. Auden.[3] Since the concept of the
greater Romantic lyric is relatively new, the list of exemplars and of
variants will undoubtedly be lengthened considerably by literary scholars
in the next decade or two, especially, we hope, in French literature. This
essay is presented as one effort in that direction.

Let us look closely at *Souvenir* to see how well it fits into the mould
of the greater Romantic lyric.

1. *An extended poem involving a description of a natural setting, an
interaction or interinvolvement between the setting and the observing
subject modulating into a sustained meditation that interweaves
perceptual, personal and philosophical elements.*

Souvenir is an extended lyric consisting of 45 quatrains, nearly three
times the number in *Le Lac*, and begins with the narrator's reaction
to a revisited natural setting.

> J'espérais bien pleurer, mais je croyais souffrir,
> En osant te revoir, place à jamais sacrée. . . .[4]
> (1-2)

As in *Tintern Abbey*, *Le Lac* and *Tristesse d'Olympio* the scene is
associated with a beloved female companion, and the secluded scene ("cette
solitude")— just as in *Tintern Abbey* — impresses "thoughts of more
deep seclusion." The narrator's friends fear that the revisitation will prove
too wrenching an experience for him.

> Que redoutiez-vous donc de cette solitude,
> Et pourquoi, mes amis, me preniez-vous la main?
> (5-6)

Perceptual and personal elements are immediately interwoven: Nature
becomes a "shrine [*tombe*] where sleeps a memory." The setting
immediately evokes the image of a former mistress.

> Les voilà, ces coteaux, ces bruyères fleuries,
> Et ces pas argentins sur le sable muet,
> Ces sentiers amoureux remplis de causeries,
> Où son bras m'enlaçait.
> (9-12)

> Ainsi de cette terre, humide encor de pluie,
> Sortent, sous tes rayons, tous les parfums du jour;
> Aussi calme, aussi pur, de mon âme attendrie
> Sort mon ancien amour.
> (37-40)

Joachim Merlant's comment on this last passage is apposite: "Musset a senti et exprimé, avec une sobriété charmante, les correspondances qui lient les états de la nature à ceux de l'âme—ici, celles qui unissent un paysage transformé par la magie nocturne à une âme apaisée d'où s'exhale le souvenir" (*Morceaux choisis*, p. 467).

The rest of the poem is a philosophical meditation, compelled by the natural scene, on the evanescence of human happiness and, as we shall see, on the essence of human life.

2. *A determinate speaker in a particularlized outdoor setting, whom we overhear as he carries on a sustained colloquy either with himself, with the outer scene or with a silent human auditor, present or absent.*

Souvenir is anchored to a specific time and place, as Patricia Ward has said of *Tintern Abbey* and *Tristesse d'Olympio*. Musset's brother Paul has related to us the particular circumstances under which the poem was written: the revisitation at Fontainebleau of a natural scene that Musset had shared seven years earlier, in 1833, with George Sand shortly before their fateful trip to Italy; the unexpected meeting with her, several months after the revisitation, at the Théâtre Italien; the feverish writing of *Souvenir* that very night.

The narrator's colloquy is carried on in the first stanza with the outer scene—

> En osant te revoir, place à jamais sacrée
> (2)

in the second stanza with silent human auditors ("mes amis") and in the third and forth stanzas with himself. At the end of the fifth stanza the poet apostrophizes Nature once again:

> Lieux charmants, beau désert qu'aimait tant ma maîtresse,
> Ne m'attendiez-vous pas?
> (19-20)

The imperative of the sixth stanza seems addressed to Nature and to the poet's worried friends addressed earlier.

> Ah! laissez-les couler, elles me sont bien chères,
> Ces larmes que soulève un coeur encor blessé!

> Ne les essuyez pas, laissez sur mes paupières
> Ce voile du passé!
> (21-24)

3. *The speaker begins with a description of the landscape; an aspect or change of aspect in the landscape evokes a varied but integral process of memory, thought, anticipation and feeling which remains closely intervolved with the outer scene.*

In *Souvenir* the sight of the heather and hillocks, the "silvery" sound of footsteps in the sand, activate the involuntary memory and produce a varied reaction. First, sweet nostalgia: the poet recalls the "fair days" of his youth; then his mistress' intense love of this particular setting; but the recollection of her subsequent betrayal brings tears to his eyes. However, a stoic pride, worthy of Vigny, prevents the poet from indulging in self-pity and recrimination.

> Je ne viens point jeter un regret inutile.
> (25)

> Que celui-là se livre à des plaintes amères,
> Qui s'agenouille et prie au tombeau d'un ami.
> (29-30)

> Loin de moi les vains mots, les frivoles pensées,
> Des vulgaires douleurs linceul accoutumé,
> Que viennent étaler sur leurs amours passées
> Ceux qui n'ont point aimé!
> (53-56)

All these varied feelings remain closely intervolved with the outer scene. In fact the interinvolvement is so close that the pathetic fallacy comes into play. The very *sentiers* which witnessed the lovers' embrace become, through a transferred epithet, *amoureux* themselves (11); and the poet's stoic pride is reinforced by the fact that Nature herself sets the example:

> Fière est cette forêt dans sa beauté tranquille,
> Et fier aussi mon coeur.
> (27-28)

4. *In the course of the meditation the lyric speaker either achieves and insight, faces up to a tragic loss, comes to a moral decision or resolves the emotional problem.*

All these thematic elements are present in *Souvenir*. The first insight gained is that Time is not only the great destroyer, as Hugo and Lamartine had complained, but also and more importantly, the great healer.

O puissance du temps! ô légères années!
Vous emportez nos pleurs, nos cris et nos regrets;
(45-46)

This thought leads the poet to pick a philosophical quarrel with Dante—

Dante, pourquoi dis-tu qu'il n'est pire misère
Qu'un souvenir heureux dans les jours de douleur?
Quel chagrin t'a dicté cette parole amère,
Cette offense au malheur?
(57-60)

and to achieve another insight: *to have been is to be*, as Georges Poulet says of Musset in *La Distance intérieure*. For Musset, as for all French romantic poets and even preromantic *prosateurs* (e.g., Rousseau, Chateaubriand and Senancour), the memory of a happy experience is more real than the original experience itself:

Un souvenir heureux est peut-être sur terre
Plus vrai que le bonheur.
(67-68)

It is more durable; it is purer in the chemical sense of being unalloyed with baser instincts and motives or bitter feelings like jealousy and revenge.

Ainsi de cette terre, humide encor de pluie,
Sortent, sous tes rayons, tous les parfums du jour;
Aussi calme, *aussi pur*, de mon âme attendrie
Sort mon ancien amour.
(37-40; emphasis added)

Here the purity of love experiences, transformed into what Robert Denommé calls "crystallized recollections," (*Romantic Poets*, pp. 134 and 139) is associated with the vibrant purity of the earth after a gentle rain, just as the "souvenir heureux" of stanza 17 is associated with the *pur flambeau* of the moon. Indeed it is Nature's "natural purity" that impels thoughts of moral purity (cf. the *vallon pur* observed by Olympio). In *Tintern Abbey* Wordsworth tells us that he finds "In nature and the language of the senses"

The anchor of my *purest* thoughts, the nurse
The guide, the guardian of my heart, and soul
Of all my moral being.
(emphasis added)

The original experience, then, is maintained through memory in its pristine, "natural" purity and also escapes the ravages of Time. Another pre-Proustian insight is that man is not the sum of all his experiences, as Malraux and the existentialists have told us, but of the privileged moments.

> Ce fugitif instant fut toute votre vie.
> (99)

This is a position diametrically opposed to the one taken by Hugo's persona at one point in *Tristesse d'Olympio*:

> N'existons-nous donc plus? Avons-nous eu notre heure?
> L'air joue avec la branche au moment où je pleure;
> Ma maison me regarde et ne me connaît plus.

At this point a bitter Olympio sees human existence as an insignificant speck in Space and Time, but he too will ultimately resolve the philosophical problem by invoking the *sacré* souvenir. As Patricia Siegel has noted ("Dante or Hugo?," p. 11), Musset surprises us by his almost cold rationality, while Hugo continues to search desperately but fruitlessly for some reassurance from Nature. Hugo's bitterness is not assuaged at the end of his poem whereas Musset yields with philosophic calm to the inevitability of change, to an ontology of becoming, thanks to the one constant in human life: the persistence of memory.

Musset arrives at his first insight at the very beginning of the poem. At first he fears that the memory educed by the revisited scene will not be "pure" but bitter-sweet; this is the meaning of the *pleurer/souffrir* nuance of "J'espérais bien pleurer, mais je croyais souffrir/En osant te revoir. . . ." But he notes with relief that no bitterness has surfaced: he can face up now to the greatest loss in his life with equanimity. The emotional problem, already under control at the beginning of the poem, is definitively resolved, and the poet will affirm a moral decision: he will forgive his unfaithful mistress and will remember the good days without bitterness.

5. *Often the poem rounds upon itself, to end where it began, at the outer scene, but with an altered mood and deepened understanding which is the result of the intervening meditation.*

After stanza 10 and for the length of 31 successive stanzas the outer scene is totally forgotten and yields to the abstract meditation. In stanza 42 the poet finally addresses Nature once again, then becomes aware once again, in the penultimate stanza, of the scene before him ("ces vastes cieux") and in the concluding stanza interweaves the setting ("ce lieu") with the treasured memory. The poem ends where it began: at the outer, "sacred" scene.

> Je me dis seulement: "A cette heure, *en ce lieu*,
> Un jour, je fus aimé, j'aimais, elle était belle.
> J'enfouis ce trésor dans mon âme immortelle,
> Et je l'emporte à Dieu!"
> (177-180; emphasis added)

The fact that the poem rounds upon itself is confirmed also by the sudden change in rhyme schemes at the end. Nearly all (41 out of 45) of the poem's quatrains have *rimes croisée*s, but the final two stanzas return to the *rimes embrassée*s used in the initial stanza. Nearly all (43 out of 45) of the quatrains begin with a feminine rhyme, but the final stanza returns to the initial masculine rhyme of the first stanza.

Musset's insistent use of the demonstrative adjective when describing or alluding to the natural scene, both at the beginning of the poem and at the end—

ces vastes lieux	cette solitude
ce lieu	cette terre
ces coteaux	ces pas argentins
ces buissons	

recalls that of Wordsworth in *Tintern Abbey*.

these waters	these pastoral farms
these steep and lofty cliffs	these beauteous forms
these orchard-tufts	this fair river
this dark sycamore	this delightful stream
these hedge-rows	

These demonstratives establish the dependence of the objects perceived upon the subjective experience of the perceiver. As Richard Haven explains:

> But of course in "Tintern Abbey" we can separate setting from speaker only by a conscious effort that violates the poem. Gray's verbs [in "Elegy Written in a Country Courtyard"] relate noun to noun; Wordsworth's relate noun to first person pronoun: "I hear," "I behold," "I view," "I see." Even when the subject of the verb is not "I," the construction still conveys a subjective relation: "cliffs,/That on a wild secluded scene *impress/Thoughts*" and "*connect* the *landscape* with the *quiet* of the sky" (5-8; italics added). The pattern is described as one which cannot exist independently of the perceiver, and it is

this which constitutes the particularity of both speaker and setting. . . . The emphasis is on the demonstrative pronouns [sic.] (*these* waters, *these* cliffs, *this* dark sycamore) which relate the nouns to the pronoun ("these where I am, which I see") rather than on the nouns themselves. ("Some Perspectives," pp. 176-77)

The demonstratives in *Souvenir* act as shifters as well as pointers: they shift the emphasis to subjective experience. The natural objects, inventoried more than described, denote not so much the outer scene in itself as events in consciousness. (The thing itself is a sign, says Derrida, and the sign itself is an absence, says Blanchot). To the romantic nature poet the ontological status of natural objects is dual, and the two components of the duality are not usually equal. Things stand there initially, but only initially, in (a) their noumenal presence, their independent and transcendent being, as things-in-themselves to be admired for themselves, disinterestedly, [but this admiration already contaminates the transcendence with the presence of an admiring observer]; however their true being resides foremost in (b) their function as pointers to human feelings and to human relationships. Here for instance is the end of *Tintern Abbey*:

> . . .*these* steep and lofty cliffs
> And *this* green pastoral landscape, were to me
> More dear, both (a) for themselves, and (b) for thy sake.

The spatial contours in *Souvenir* are vague, not because Musset, any more than Lamartine, is an inadequate Nature poet, but because this is not a true descriptive poem but one of revery and meditation—a greater Romantic lyric. Georges Poulet has noted (*Les Métamorphoses du cercle*) that Lamartinian space is only initially and imperfectly the locus of material and concrete things. Ultimately, inevitably, in poem after poem, things retreat. This is also true of *Souvenir* in which after stanza 10 the numerous objects focussed on earlier effect a strategic withdrawal in order to allow the ideas, for which the things are mainly signs, to occupy stage center. And this is why Musset, like Wordsworth and Lamartine, attaches vague, general epithets to his nouns even when, at the beginning and at the end of his poem, he does focus on the natural objects. The demonstrative adjectives are as operative as the vague descriptive ones, and properly so.

Tintern Abbey	*Le Lac*	*Souvenir*
THESE pastoral farms	rocs sauvages	CES bruyères fleuries

THIS dark sycamore	noirs sapins	CES sapins à la sombre verdure
THESE beauteous forms	beau lac	CETTE forêt dans sa beauté tranquille
THESE steep and lofty cliffs	CES roches profondes	Cette gorge profonde
THIS delightful stream	riants coteaux	CES sentiers amoureux
	CETTE pierre où tu la vis s'asseoir	CETTE vallée amie

If Wordsworth, Lamartine and Musset had filled their poems with sharp detail, with the perfervid precision of an amateur botanist, this would have detracted, in my view, from the meditative mood. Nature, again, is not being admired, it is being examined philosophically. The demonstrative adjectives, for instance, point not so much to the beauty of the natural objects perceived by an admiring subject as to an essential and mysterious coalescence of subject-object.

Another device that points to this subject-object coalesence is the apostrophe to this "place à jamais sacrée." Abrams' essay on the greater Romantic lyric does not discuss apostrophe, although, as Jonathan Culler has pointed out, it is a prominent feature of most of the poems Abrams studies. The reason for this may be, as Culler has further suggested, that "one might be justified in taking apostrophe as the figure of all that is most radical, embarrassing, pretentious and mystificatory in the lyric" (*Pursuit of Signs*, p. 137). One function of apostrophe is to serve as an intensifier, the sign of invested passion (Fontanier). Another function of apostrophe is to serve as sign of a genre (lyric, epic, ode, and in general the sublime). Culler has identified a third function of apostrophe that is germane to a discussion of the romantic lyric in particular:

> In these terms the function of apostrophe would be to make the objects of the universe potentially responsive forces: forces which can be asked to act or refrain from acting, or even to continue behaving as they usually behave. The apostrophizing poet identifies his universe as a world of sentient forces. (p. 138)

> If, as we tend to assume, post-enlightenment poetry seeks to overcome the alienation of subject from object, then apostrophe takes the crucial step of constituting the object as another subject with whom the poet might hope to strike up a harmonious relationship. Apostrophe would figure this reconciliation of subject and object. (p. 143).

Another sign of an altered mood or deepened understanding at the very end of *Souvenir* is the sudden and somewhat surprising religious note. If one discounts the figurative (i.e., seemingly secularized) epithet "sacré" of the first stanza and the angry expletive "juste Dieu" of stanza 21, it is not only the sole religious one but also the very last note sounded in the poem, occupying thus a singularly privileged position. A man's treasured memories remain with him, Musset tells us at the end, not just for the length of his mortal days but throughout a God-governed eternity. Memories of privileged moments form, then, not only the very center of worldly existence but of the other-worldly paradise, the soul's immortal consciousness.

> Ton âme est immortelle, et va s'en souvenir.
> (*Lettre à M. de Lamartine*)

This is quite different from the treatment that God receives in *Tristesse d'Olympio* from Hugo, who a bit later in his career will conceive of himself as the poet *vates* and who will write "sous la dictée d'en haut" (Sartre). In Hugo's poem God is not depicted as the guardian of sacred memory but as the very instrument of oblivion.

> Dieu nous prête un moment les prés et les fontaines,
> Les grands bois frissonnants, les rocs profonds et sourds,
> Et les cieux azurés et les lacs et les plaines,
> Pour y mettre nos coeurs, nos rêves, nos amours;
>
> Puis il nous les retire. Il souffle notre flamme.
> Il plonge dans la nuit l'antre où nous rayonnons;
> Et dit à la vallée, où s'imprime notre âme,
> D'effacer notre trace et d'*oublier* nos noms.
> (emphasis added)

Why in *Souvenir* this sudden reference to God from a writer who in poetry, fiction and drama expresses a metaphysical anguish arising from his age's loss of faith—and his own—and who at bottom is much less a religious soul than Hugo? Surely it is not a facile device designed to elicit from the reader a stock response to the only-God-can-make-a-tree sentiment. This is simply not Musset's style. I think the best answer may be found in Georges Poulet's discussion of the romantic consciousness. If the first impulse of the man of sensibility is to be receptive to new sensations *from* the outside (despite the centrality of the self in romantic literature, consciousness of objects precedes self-consciousness, especially and necessarily when the emotion experienced is romantic love), his second impulse is to communicate these feelings *to* the external world: the movement now is from the center, the self, to the periphery.

> L'âme humaine est conçue comme un foyer d'impressions qui rayonnent au-dehors. . . Tout sentiment cherche à s'épandre et à se communiquer. Comment sentir, sans éprouver le besoin de faire partager à toutes les sensibilités périphériques les émotions ressenties d'abord au centre?
> (*Métamorphoses du cercle*, p. 133)

> Chaque heure de l'existence, chaque lieu, si ténu qu'il soit, occupé par la moindre présence, devient un centre d'énergie irradiante, qui, comme dit Saint-Martin, "croît à la fois et dans tous les sens; occupe et remplit toutes les parties de sa circonférence.

> Chaque point de la création, chaque moment particulier de la durée, révèle [for Romantics like William Blake just as for the poets of the Renaissance] une capacité d'expansion véritablement infinie. (Ibid., p. 139)

For Musset, not every but *any* hour of existence, any privileged moment or "sacred" place, can become an irradiating center capable of infinite expansion:

> Ce fugitif instant fut toute votre vie.
>   . . .
>   To see a World in a Grain of Sand
> And a Heaven in a Wild Flower,
> Hold Infinity in the palm of your hand
> And Eternity in an hour.

This is basically a religious idea, which links Musset (despite certain critical clichés to the contrary) to the mainstream of European romanticism.

> Presque simultanément, en France, en Allemagne, en Angleterre, les romantiques découvraient ou retrouvaient le caractère essentiellement religieux de la centralité humaine: "Je suis le point central, la source sainte" chante Astralis dans le roman de Novalis. L'homme est source, et source sacrée. Dans la profondeur de sa centralité se mêlent de façon indescriptible le mystère de son être et celui du Dieu qui s'y veut associer.
> (Poulet, *Métamorphoses*, p. 138)

What Poulet calls "the explosion of the center" suggests not only the sacredness of the Self, but an ever-widening periphery, the romantic quest for the Absolute. But there is also in *Souvenir*, I think, an idea of implosion, a bursting inward to the center's center, to its mysterious, essential and sacred core. This is why Olympio too will cry out that his memory is "sacred." One must read Musset's *place à jamais sacrée* as presenting not simply a conventional epithet used as a trite compliment to a former mistress, but as expressive of a genuine if unorthodox religious feeling. The God of many a romantic is not the transcendent God but the one within—

> ... non pas un Dieu extérieur, objectif, travaillant au bon fonctionnement de sa Providence externe, mais le Dieu plus intérieur à nous-mêmes que nous-mêmes et plus central que nous ne le pourrions jamais devenir. (Ibid.)

*
* *

My conclusion is brief and obvious. I have not forced Musset's *Souvenir* into the mould of the greater Romantic lyric: we are dealing here, just as much as with *Tintern Abbey, Tristesse d'Olympio* and *Le Lac*, with a perfect fit.

chapter eight
MUSICALITY AND EUPHONY

Musset was a genuine music lover and an occasional music critic. His first love was Italian music, the operas of Rossini especially; later, under the influence of George Sand, he came to appreciate the Germans, especially Mozart, Beethoven and Weber. His intense love of music is often expressed in his work, and his work, in turn, has been a source of inspiration to many musical composers, who have written over 650 pieces, from simple melodies to ballet scores, based on texts of Musset.[1]

Musset was highly conscious of the affinities between poetry and music. In this regard he was a forerunner of the Symbolists, especially Verlaine: "La poésie est si essentiellement musicale qu'il n'y a pas de si belle pensée devant laquelle le poète ne recule si la mélodie ne s'y trouve pas" (*OEuvres complètes*, p. 650). And, anticipating Baudelaire and Rimbaud, he was conscious of the synesthetic qualities of sound:

> J'ai été très fâché aujourd'hui, dînant avec ma famille, d'être obligé de soutenir une discussion pour prouver que le fa était jaune et le sol rouge (par rapport à l'arc en ciel) et de plus qu'une voix de soprano (féminin) était blonde, et qu'une voix de contralto était brune. Il me semble que ces choses-là vont sans dire.
> (Quoted by P. Reboul, "Sur cinq à six marches," p. 634.)

He also anticipated Mallarmé's poetics, stating that about 75% of poetry (Mallarmé used the same percentage) is suggestiveness, which is the most important affinity the Symbolists saw between poetry and music: "Dans tout vers remarquable d'un vrai poète, il y a deux ou trois fois plus que ce qui est dit; c'est au lecteur à suppléer le reste, selon ses idées, sa force, ses goûts" (*OEuvres complètes*, p. 650).

The musical structure and strategies of many of Musset's poems has caught the eye of of a number of critics. Anne Greet ("Humor in Musset," p. 161) has shown how Musset uses enjambement not just to startle the bourgeois and the classicist but for musical reasons: a word or phrase is of course given special emphasis, but the entire line is also affected; it is given an offbeat by having a phrase or an accent placed where it is musically unexpected. She has also shown how he plays with mute *e*'s to produce syncopation. A form of syncopation is also achieved in pieces like "Venise," "Stances," and "Ballade à la lune" by having a very short verse follow a longer one. Ladislas Galdi ("Style poétique de Musset," p. 28) speaks of Musset's use of disjunction in "Stances" as a rhetorical device (*retardatio*); but one can also speak here of melodic tension, the expected phrase (e.g., a direct object group) being postponed well beyond its normal musical as well as syntactic "slot." Maurice Toesca ("Musset ou l'amour. . . ," p. 264) says of a passage from "Sur la paresse:" "Sur ce thème Musset brode de brillants arpèges—harmoniques du passé, qui se termine par une strette" and of "Le Mie Prigione:" "Musset se répète. La musique a ce privilège: il suffit d'un dièze ou d'un bémol pour diversifier la sensation" (p. 289). Jean Cassou: "Et que de musique dans les *Nuits,* que de thèmes et de mouvements, que de grondements, que de retours de douceurs et de silence, quels apaisements délicats!" ("*Les Nuits,*" p. 126). Jean Giraud: "La composition de cette Nuit [*La Nuit d'Octobre*] est toute musicale. Les premiers vers doivent se dire 'pianissimo'" (p. 122). Charles Fournet ("Poètes romantiques," p. 95) has noted the "harmonieux phrasé musical" of *Souvenir* and affirms that "Ce Musset-là est tout proche de Lamartine." Gautier-Ferrières (*Musset,* p. 26): "Il sait la valeur des syllabes sourdes ou sonores, et, par leur emploi bien approprié, abrège ou prolonge à son gré la résonance d'un vers." Emile Montégut (*Nos Morts,* p. 300) calls Musset "le plus musical des poètes." Jean Giraud has noted the musical structure of "Simone," "Lucie" and *A la Malibran,* especially the repetition of the initial theme in a coda. And in chapter two I pointed out contrapuntal arrangements in *A quoi rêvent les jeunes filles?* and *Rolla* and, in *Rolla* again, musical amplifications and variations on an initial theme. It might be stretching a point, but one might analyze the structure of *Namouna* in terms of a musical fugue, with the introduction of themes followed by whimsical and later, serious, repetitions of the themes in contrasting but parallel variations.

There are many passages in Musset's poetry that seem ready made for music. Pierre Gastinel speaks of a scene in the second act of *A quoi rêvent* as a kind of *chant alterné*; it is indeed, as I suggested earlier, a lovely duet.

NINON

Toi dont la voix est douce, et douce la parole,
Chanteur mystérieux, reviendras-tu me voir?
Ou, comme en soupirant l'hirondelle s'envole,
Mon bonheur fuira-t-il, n'ayant duré qu'un soir?

NINETTE

Audacieux fantôme à la forme voilée,
Les ombrages ce soir seront-ils sans danger?

Te reverrai-je encor dans cette sombre allée,
Ou disparaîtras-tu comme un chamois léger?

NINON
L'eau, la terre et les vents, tout s'emplit d'harmonies.
Un jeune rossignol chante au fond de mon coeur.
J'entends sous les roseaux murmurer des génies. . .
Ai-je de nouveaux sens inconnus à ma soeur?

NINETTE
Pourquoi ne puis-je voir sans plaisir et sans peine
Les baisers du zéphyr trembler sur la fontaine?
Et l'ombre des tilleuls passer sur mes bras nus?
Ma soeur est une enfant, et je ne le suis plus.

Gastinel's commentary is apposite: "La scène entière, par vers séparés, par quatrains, puis deux vers à deux vers, balance ainsi, sur un rhythme identique, deux pensées qui progressent du même pas. Peut-on rêver poésie plus musicale? Ni enjambement, ni césure irrégulière, ni souci de la rime riche. Mais une recherche des sonorités, une volonté d'évoquer des images par les sons, l'art de l'harmonie légère. Il n'y a rien là qui ne soit presque impalpable, et l'on pense à la fois à l'harmonie classique et au conseil de Verlaine:

De la musique avant toute chose
De la musique encore et toujours.

En effet, Musset ici et désormais, recherche surtout la musique du vers" (*Romantisme de Musset*, pp. 270-71).

At the beginning of *La Nuit de Mai* the poet and the Muse engage in counterpoint. The Muse offers the opening theme.

Poète, prends ton luth et me donne un baiser.

The Poet is as yet unaware of the Muse's presence and displays another mood entirely:

Comme il fait noir dans la vallée!

The thematic contrast is underscored by the shorter line and the exclamatory tone. The difference in texture of the two juxaposed passages is quite arresting. Then the Muse restates the initial theme.

Poète, prends ton luth; la nuit, sur la pelouse,
Balance le zéphyr dans son voile odorant.

The Poet begins to sense her presence.

> Pourquoi mon coeur bat-il si vite?
>
> . . .
>
> Qui vient? qui m'appelle?

The seriated interrogatives provide melodic contrast to the Muse's declaratives and preparation for a change of theme. Then follows still another restatement of the initial theme.

> Poète, prends ton luth; le vin de la jeunesse
> Fermente cette nuit dans les veines de Dieu.

The Poet is now close to recognizing Her.

> Est-ce toi dont la voix m'appelle,
> O ma pauvre Muse! est-ce toi?

Then the question becomes an affirmation and an exclamation scored *fortissimo*.

> C'est toi, ma maîtresse et ma soeur!

I submit that this is a musical progression. Theme and counter-theme are presented separately, as they must be in poetry, but they follow each so closely that the thematic simultaneity of counterpoint is approximated. Then there is the gradual rapprochement of Muse and Poet in this overture that allows the former to begin the first long statement with her fourth entry. The musical structure aids in interpreting the major theme: although it is the poet who sounds the text's last note, a despondent one, his part is tentative compared to that of the Muse: it is she who provides the dominant mood and theme, marked *allegro appassionato*.

The roles are reversed in *La Nuit d'Août*: the poet not only has the last word, but his finale comes in a longer passage marked by longer phrasing (the twelve-syllable line). This is nothing tentative now: he orchestrates his theme with ringing repetitions.

> Puisque, jusqu'aux rochers, tout se change en poussière;
> Puisque tout meurt ce soir pour revivre demain;
> Puisque c'est un engrais que le meurtre et la guerre;
> Puisque sur une tombe on voit sortir de terre
> Le brin d'herbe sacré qui nous donne le pain;
>
> O Muse! que m'importe ou la mort ou la vie?
> J'aime, et je veux pâlir; j'aime et je veux souffrir;
> J'aime, et pour un baiser je donne mon génie;
> J'aime, et je veux sentir sur ma joue amaigrie
> Ruisseler une source impossible à tarir.

The structural design of these lines offers the rigid symmetry, the nearly mathematical architectonics of a coda.

Lila Maurice-Amour puts well the importance of music in Musset's poetry: "L'oeuvre entière de Musset est toute baignée de musique. Elle n'y apparaît pas comme un élément décoratif, une coloration fugitive: elle y est présente, incorporée à la substance poétique" ("Musset, musique. . . ," p. 34).

While some critics, like Pierre Gastinel, admire the "harmony" of Musset's regular rhythms, others, like Valentine Brunet, find the source of Musset's musical genius in his irregular, off-beat rhythms.

> C'est par l'association inattendue de groupes irréguliers que le poète manifeste la fantaisie de son imagination musicale. Il rend ainsi, sans se donner la peine de les chercher, mais par un instinct impérieux de sa nature, des tonalités très nuancées comme le musicien trouve dans des associations de notes les sons qui correspondent à ses états d'âme. (*Lyrisme de Musset*, p. 508)

Even after his first manner, when Musset was no longer trying so self-consciously to dislocate the alexandrine, his verse is often characterized by fluid rhythms created not only by enjambement and irregular *coupes* but also irregular rhyme and stanza patterns. While he quickly abandoned his interest in rhythmic virtuosity for its own sake, he continued to criticize the monotonous rhythms of the neoclassical alexandrine which marched side by side with exactly similar ones "like oxen in the furrow" (*Namouna*). One remedy he found was to alternate the alexandrine with other meters in the same passage; with the octo-syllable for example—

> Jours de travail! seuls jours où j'ai vécu!
> O trois fois chère solitude!
> (*Nuit d'Octobre*)

or the six-syllable line: in "Vision," for example, the poet gives us the following pattern: 12-6-12-12-6. In "La Chanson espagnole" the alexandrine comes simply as a musical contrast to danse rhythms: 8-6-8-8/5-5-5-5/8-2-12. In "Conseils à une Parisienne" the decasyllable is followed by a 2-syllable line. The octosyllable is frequently united with a four-syllable line and in "Réponse à Charles Nodier" it is joined with a line of just three syllables.

In a good number of poems there is probably more to these irregular patterns than fluidity, syncopation and variation. Musset seems at times to be striving for *musique imitative*. Valentine Brunet and Maurice

Grammont are the only critics who have stressed this aspect of Musset's style. Let me give a few concrete examples. Of the following lines

> Toi qui regardes au loin le pâtre qui chemine
> Tandis que pas à pas son long troupeau le suit. . .

Brunet (p. 62) says: "Ces deux vers contiennent un tableau des plus poétiques et une musique imitative qui fait longtemps rêver." She doesn't really explain, but I gather she sees a connection between the slow-moving shepherd and flock on the one hand and the poetic rhythm on the other. She finds (p. 508) that the alternation of a decasyllable and octosyllable in *La Nuit d'Octobre* gives the lines "la douceur d'une rêverie et d'une confidence." In the "Réponse à Charles Nodier" she finds the combination of octosyllable with the three-syllable line evocative of the ambivalent nostalgia of which the poem speaks. The 8-8-4 sequence in another passage "nous donne," she says, "l'impression d'un pas que la tristesse écourte, d'une marche qui s'arrête tout à coup sous le poids du souvenir ou de la souffrance" (ibid.). In "Conseils à une Parisienne" the mixture of long and short verses suggests to her the small talk during the *contredanse*, that is, the flitting from one frivolous subject to another, the teasing, the flattery and also the danse step itself.

One needs to take all this with caution. What Maurice Grammont (*Le vers français*, p. 127) has said of sounds should also be said of rhythms: they are only potentially expressive; it is the semantic value of the words being used that allows sounds and rhythms to realize their expressive potential. We *can* say with some assurance that Musset does use rhythms, not to evoke directly, but to *suggest*, or at least reinforce, certain images and certain ideas. Thus Brunet is on safer ground when she says that the mixture of the alexandrine with the six-syllable line in "Vision" is "appropriate" to the theme: "cet état de sommeil, et, pourtant, de conscience, qui est le propre des rêves dont nous gardons un souvenir ineffaçable" (p. 509).

Asserting that "la poésie est essentiellement suggestive," Maurice Grammont, like Brunet, has studied *musique imitative* in Musset, concentrating on sounds rather than rhythms. I shall give just a few of his numerous examples.

A repeated phoneme can give the impression of the repeated movement of a machine—few would disagree with Grammont here.

> L'horloge d'un couvent s'ébranla lentement.
> (Don Paez)

A repeated *voyelle aiguë* can evoke a light, rapid movement or *élan*.

> Oh! si j'avais des ailes
> Vers ce beau ciel si pur je voudrais les ouvrir.
> > (*Rolla*)

Likewise the *voyelles graves* in

> Mais il y pend toujours quelques gouttes de sang.
> > (*Nuit de Mai*)

are expressive of the grave idea being enunciated. When Musset emphasizes the nasal vowels (*voyelles voilées*), he usually wants to underscore notions of slowness, langour, indolence, softness, nonchalance.

> Et du fond des boudoirs les belles indolentes
> Balançant mollement leurs tailles nonchalantes
> > ("A la Mi-Carême")

Musset will use consonants as well as vowels for their *musique imitative*. Unvoiced plosives are used to suggest "dry" or jerky movements or to spit out bitter, sarcastic irony:

> Dors-tu content, Voltaire, et ton hideux sourire
> Voltige-t-il encor sur tes os décharnés?
> Ton siècle était, dit-on, trop jeune pour te lire;
> Le nôtre doit te plaire, et tes hommes sont nés.
> Il est tombé sur nous, cet édifice immense
> Que de tes larges mains tu sapais nuit et jour.
> La Mort devait t'attendre avec impatience,
> Pendant quatre vingts ans que tu lui fis ta cour;
> > (*Rolla*)

Such an intention could explain the substitution of "*ta* cour" for "*la* cour." The thirty unvoiced plosives in the above passage are seconded by fourteen other sounds: the voiced *d*, the sibilant *s* and the fricative *f*.

Thus far I have discussed musicality in Musset in terms of expressiveness. I shall now turn to a more delicate subject: euphony.

*
* *

In a preliminary study, "Phonological Correlates of Euphony," I attempted, with the aid of examples from the poetry of Paul Verlaine, to demonstrate the underlying principles of "laws" of euphony.[2] During the course of the demonstration, I had occasion to criticize the method of analysis of the leading French authority on the subject, Maurice Grammont, on both theoretical and practical grounds. I have since refined my methods and am ready to challenge Grammont on his own ground by studying euphony in Musset, a poet Grammont himself analyzed in great detail.

In *Le Lyrisme d'Alfred de Musset* Valentine Brunet frequently refers to the musicality and melodiousness of Musset's poetry, but her analyses, although she does on one occasion mention the importance of the "sounds," do not go beyond the study of rhythm. I believe that she is responding, at least at times, to something besides the rhythms; this something else, this *certain je ne sais quoi*, is euphony. And the fact that Grammont selected Musset as one of the six poets upon whom he constructed his theory and method suggests that he too considers much of Musset's verse to be euphonious. Musset is indeed a poet for whom euphony is important: "Il n'y a pas de si belle pensée devant laquelle le poète ne recule si la mélodie ne s'y trouve pas."

Grammont refers to euphony as *harmonie* and *la musique du vers*. Other French critics refer to it as *musique pure* as distinguished from *musique imitative*. Grammont claims that euphony is produced solely by the "notes" in the line, that is, the vowels: "Il faut que ces voyelles se suivent dans un certain ordre: voilà tout le secret de l'harmonie du vers français" (*Le vers français*, p. 381). He goes on to say that euphony results strictly from the correspondences (i.e., similar vocalic patterns) between vowels grouped in twos (*dyades*) or threes (*triades*) or multiples of two (*tétrades*) and three (*hexades*). Different combinations of these systems can be found in the same line. A delicate and well trained ear perceives these correspondences if the groups follow each other directly or are disposed symmetrically. If there are no such correspondences between groups, there is no euphony.

What determines the groups? The ear, which is guided by the main divisions in the lines, the *coupes* or rhythmic groups. The most harmonious verses are those whose vowel groups coincide with the rhythmic groups, repeat the same patterns found in other groups within the same line and meet two other conditions:[3]

> 1. They exhibit "modulation," which for Grammont simply means change, preferably a mixture of *voyelles claires* (those whose point of articulation is near the front of the palate) and *voyelles graves* (all the others). If all three vowels in a triad are *graves*, there should be modulation from *sombres* (*o* and *u*) to *éclatantes* (a, ʊ, œ). If all three vowels are *claires*,

there should be modulation between *aiguës* (*i* and *y*) and
non-aigües (e, ε, φ.) In Racine's line—

Vous mourûtes aux bords où vous fûtes laissée.

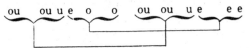

—the first, third and fourth triads exhibit exemplary
modulation between *graves* and *claires* with the first and
third reproducing each other exactly. The second triad
contains only *graves*, but there is modulation within the class
between *éclatantes* and *sombres*.

2. To be perceptible to the ear, groups having similar patterns
should be juxtaposed or else be disposed symmetrically within
the line, e.g., triads that reproduce the same pattern "deux
à deux" like *rimes plates* or "de deux en deux" like *rimes
croisées* or "en chiasme" like *rimes embrassées*. An example
of the latter:

Tout m'afflige et me nuit et conspire à me nuire.

    ggc   cgc   cgc   ggc

Using this system, Grammont tested hundreds of lines from six poets—
Racine, Hugo, Musset, Leconte de Lisle, Boileau and Lamartine—and
rated them in that order from the point of view of lines exhibiting "bonne
harmonie:" from 42% for Racine and Hugo to 33% for Lamartine, with
Musset ranking third with 38%. Musset fares well in this illustrious group.
His placement ahead of Lamartine may come as a surprise since the
latter's poetry has been more noted for euphony than Musset's, at least
in school manuals. Another surprise is that Grammont found only one
third of Lamartine's lines showing "good harmony." If 77% of Lamartine's
lines do not offer *bonne harmonie*, it is difficult to see how he can be
classified as a writer of euphonious verse. Either Lamartine's poetry is
not very euphonious—despite a broad critical consensus that it *is*
euphonious—or Grammont's system is not very accurate.

In my view there is more to euphony in Musset's poetry (and that
of any other poet) than corresponding groups of modulated vowels, and
I believe that the percentage of euphonic lines in Musset is much higher
than Grammont's system reveals. In "Phonological Correlates of
Euphony" I take issue with Grammont on several specific points.

1. I believe that consonants as well as vowels play a significant role in euphony. We know that vowels, with their free flow of air, have a much higher sonority than consonants, ranging between 9 and 47 when measured in microwatts, whereas consonants range only between 0.08 and 2.11.[4] And all vowels, unlike many consonants, are accompanied by vibration of the vocal chords and are thus given an additional resonance. However, when consonants are arranged in certain patterns, they can have more than a mere percussive role to play in the "harmony" of the poetic line.

2. Grammont expels from the domain of euphony lines of uneven-numbered syllables and of fewer than eight syllables (which explains his surprising omission of Verlaine in a discussion of euphony). But to disregard short verses must be considered a purely personal choice; it is mere typography for instance that keeps two four-syllable lines from forming an octosyllable. A dislike of asymmetrical rhythm may even be an unmusical idea. Northrop Frye has pointed out that true musical rhythm is not characterized by a sing-song regularity (as, say, in the nursery rhyme) and declares that "the rhythm and rhyme that tend to make the single line a unit in itself are unmusical" (*Sound and Poetry*, p. xv). French poetry, then, was made *more* musical by the introduction of the displaced caesura and by run-on and uneven lines. I am not confusing (i.e., fusing) euphony and music. The latter, as Frye has noted, is not primarily concerned with the "beauty" of sound but with the organization of sound. But there is a valid analogy between euphony and one of music's most important aspects: melody or linear harmony.

3. In isolating patterns that contribute to euphony Grammont claims that they cannot cut across the main pause, whereas I feel that certain euphonic patterns develop over a whole poetic line (e.g., alliteration and assonance) and even from line to line (e.g., rhyme, refrain and anaphora—all of which, by the way, involve consonants).

4. Whereas Grammont would emphasize the felicitous "modulation" with a group such as $i\ \tilde{a}\ i$—that is, from a close or high front vowel to an open or low back vowel, and back again—I believe that if such a sequence were repeated frequently at short distance, any sense of euphony would be lessened or even cancelled out by the feeling of *effort*, since the tongue is forced to move rapidly over a relatively large distance from one vowel to an unrelated one, and since the widely held presumption is that there is a positive correlation between lingual ease and aural pleasure.

Before presenting my findings with regard to Musset, I must first present my own views on the subject of euphony. After examination of a large number of lines of Paul Verlaine judged to be euphonious by an impressive consensus of critics, translators and fellow poets, I came to the conclusion several years ago that there are three basic principles or "laws" of euphony: identity, proximity and progression.

*

* *

I. IDENTITY. This principle needs little commentary since most critics agree that repetition of the same sounds in rhyme, refrain, assonance and alliteration, if not overdone, is intrinsically euphonious: this is one of the many aesthetic pleasures offered by poetry. The analogy with music is obvious: music without repetition would be reduced to the fascinating twentieth-century experiments in dissonance such as atonalism and the twelve-tone scale, in which not only repetition is avoided but where the melodic line jumps from one note to a non-harmonic one. The first stanza of Verlaine's "Chanson d'automne" provides an example of the use of repetition to achieve euphony.

> Les sanglots longs
> Des violons
> De l'automne
>
> Blessent mon coeur
> D'une langueur
> Monotone.

In these lines the triple slant assonance in *o* (involving open, close and nasal *o*'s) is reinforced by something Grammont considers inoperative "musically:" the alliteration in *l*. In addition to the alliteration and assonance, Verlaine exploits the euphonious potential of the short poetic line, which brings the rhymes closer together.[5] So does Musset.

In his "Poems to be set to Music" (from the *Contes d'Espagne et d'Italie*). Musset experiments with the short, six-syllable line to bring the rhymes closer together and will often insert even shorter lines for the same effect and also, perhaps, to produce syncopation, as suggested earlier.

> Dans Venise la rouge
> Pas un bateau qui bouge
> Pas un pêcheur dans l'eau
> Pas un falot.

In "Stances" and "Le Lever" the short line reinforces rich rhyme:

> J'aime vos tours à tête grise
> Où se brise
> L'éclair avec la brise.

Repetition reaches its zenith in two stanzas of "Venise:" the rich rhyme at the end of the first one is reinforced by the polysyndeton and anaphora of the beginning; words that are not involved in repetition are completely engulfed by words that are—in fact the engulfed words are linked by slant assonance: a-sounds in one stanza and o-sounds in the other.

> Et les palais antiques,
> Et les graves portiques,
> Et les blancs escaliers
> Des chevaliers,
>
> Et les ponts et les rues,
> Et les mornes statues,
> Et le golfe mouvant
> Qui tremble au vent.

Throughout Musset's entire poetic career, he will use repetition with insistence in the service of euphony. Here is a non-exhaustive list of short poems with short lines that involve many repetitions in addition to the rhymes: "Chanson" ("A Saint-Blaise. . ."); "Chanson de Barberine"; "Chanson de Fortunio"; "Le Mie Prigione"; "Rappelle-toi"; "Mimi Pinson"; "Réponse à Charles Nodier"; "A mon frère, revenant d'Italie"; "Cantate de Bettine"; "Les Filles de Madrid"; "Chanson" ("Bonjour, Suzon"); "La Nuit"; "L'Anglaise en diligence"; "Le petit moinillon." In the first poem on the list it is clear that Musset is more concerned with sound than sense:

> A Saint-Blaise, à la Zuecca,
> Vous étiez, vous étiez bien aise
>   A Saint-Blaise.
> A Saint-Blaise, à la Zuecca,
>   Nous étions bien là.

Some of these poems juxtapose repeated phrases as above.

> Mimi Pinson est une blonde.
> Une blonde qui. . .
>   ******
> Ne me fais pas, je t'en conjure,
> Cette injure

De supposer que j'ai faibli
Par oubli.
L'oubli. . .

Others use insistent rhyme schemes (for instance, aaab/cccb in "Cantate
de Bettine") or insistent refrain (sometimes with effective variations as
in "Adieux à Suzon" and "Sur une Morte"). The repetition of entire
lines is used most frequently in "Le petit moinillon."

Charmant petit moinillon blanc,
Je suis un pauvre mendiant.
Charmant petit moinillon rose,
Je vous demande peu de chose.
Accordez-le-moi poliment,
Charmant petit moinillon blanc.

Charmant petit moinillon rose,
En vous tout mon espoir repose.
Charmant petit moinillon blanc,
Parfois l'espoir est décevant.
Je voudrais parler mais je n'ose,
Charmant petit moinillon rose.

And so on for ten more stanzas.

In longer poems with longer lines, the decasyllable and alexandrine,
Musset will frequently use anaphora not just for the crescendo effect (as
in the declamatory style of *La Coupe et les Lèvres*), not just for comic
and ironic effect (as in the first canto of *Namouna*) but for euphony.
In the second canto of *Namouna* (Sainte-Beuve, who had praised the
sons mélodieux of Musset's verse, considered this second canto to rank
among the greatest moments of French poetry; this apparent
overestimation may be in part the result of euphony), which is serious
in tone and at times lyrical, anaphora is used with increasing frequency.
There are more than a dozen passages in which it is used in *Rolla*. In
La Nuit de Mai and *La Nuit d'Août*, it is the Muse, who has the longer
lines, that uses anaphora. In the final section of the latter poem, the
Poet will finally be given the longer lines to express his triumphant
credo of love. Here anaphora will be used not just to enhance the rhetorical
emphasis of the extremely long periodic sentence, but for harmony in
its own right.

Puisque l'oiseau des bois voltige et chante encore,
. . .
Puisque la fleur des champs entr'ouverte à l'aurore, . . .
Puisqu' au fond des forêts, sous les toits de verdure,
. . .

Et puisqu'en traversant l'immortelle nature

. . .

Puisque, jusqu'aux rochers, tout se change en poussière;
Puisque tout meurt ce soir pour revivre demain;
Puisque c'est un engrais que le meurtre et la guerre;
Puisque sur une tombe on voit sortir de terre
Le brin d'herbe sacré qui nous donne le pain;

O Muse! que m'importe ou la mort ou la vie?
J'aime, et je veux pâlir; j'aime et je veux souffrir;
J'aime, et pour un baiser je donne mon génie;
J'aime et je veux sentir sur ma joue amaigrie
Ruisseler une source impossible à tarir.

Other poems in which anaphora is used for euphony as well as for rhetorical effect are *Lettre à M. de Lamartine, L'Espoir en Dieu, Souvenir* and especially "A Ninon," "Rappelle-toi" and "Le treize juillet."

As it is with aesthetic pleasure in general, euphony depends upon a recognition of order (pattern, structure) being imposed on chaos: even without the interval of silence, one knows when the orchestra has ceased tuning up. The least subtle and most easily recognizable pattern, in both music and poetry, is repetition. Whether repetition satisfies a deep-rooted intellectual thirst for unity, or order, or the pleasure of recognition itself, or whether it is an outgrowth of the psychological tendency of intense emotions to express themselves in throbbing litanies, we can only surmise. One thing is sure: it works. Repetition is so obvious a device that the perceptive reader can be simultaneously aware both of the pleasurable effect and the probable cause. As we move gradually farther away from repetition, with proximity and progression, the *sense* of recognition persists, that is, euphony remains within the threshold of perception (we agree with Michael Riffaterre that there can be no true stylistic effect beyond this threshold), but the reader will not be able to put his finger on what patterns are working on him (on his behalf) except through rather rigorous re-reading, that is, analysis.

*

* *

II. PROXIMITY. The use of repetition, or what I am calling the principle of identity, is well known. What has not been fully studied is the use of related phonemes—a talent shared by all, or most, born poets. There is in euphony not only the pleasure of recognition but also an articulatory pleasure experienced when one utters sounds produced in the same vicinity. As André Spire notes: "Tandis qu'en musique les affinités des sons semblent avoir pour cause des propriétés purement musicales. . . . ces accords ou désaccords de phonèmes se produisent en fonction de la position des organes buccaux qui les émettent, bref de leurs points d'articulation" (*Plaisir poétique*, p. 200). Professor Frohock's analysis of Verlaine's "Chanson d'automne" is also relevant here, lending support to our principle of proximity.

> The sounds are juxtaposed in several places in such a way that they are pronounced with the same mouth opening and in nearly the same position in the mouth: for example, in the first stanza we pass from closed *o* in *glots* to a nasal *o* which is open. The same pattern is repeated in the second, and in the third the closed *o* (spelled *au*) is followed by an open *o* which is not nasalized. And similar procedures make the rhyme richer in one place than the reader would at first suspect: the *coeur-gueur* rhyme uses initial palatal sounds. . . which, while not entirely identical, are articulated very much in the same way. The feeling of ease experienced in pronouncing such verses may come from the fact that few muscular gymnastics are required, so that one seems to modulate from one sound to another. (*Close Reading*, p. 59)

Note that Frohock uses the term *modulation* to denote, not mere change, as does Grammont, but gradual change from one sound to an adjacent one, that is, proximity.

Here is another obvious example of proximity from Verlaine:

Et mes pieds offensés que Madeleine baigne.

The euphonious effect of the variations on the e-theme is intensified by the rhythmical symmetry of the four accented vowels. The syncopation caused by the three non-elided "mute" *e*'s in the second hemistitch, a frequent device in Verlaine's poetry, gives added force to the already tonic open *e*'s. The final *e*, although theoretically mute in both recitation and scansion, is actually part of the pattern and may deserve more than a parenthesis.

In the following lines—

> Et je m'en vais
> Au vent mauvais
> Qui m'emporte

—in addition to the rhyme and the assonance in nasal-*a* there is an interplay of open and close *e*'s, of open and close *o*'s, and also of bilabial and labiodental consonants (the *m*'s and *v*'s). The use of proximal phonemes is subtler than rhyme or assonance and alliteration but yields an analogous sense of ease and harmony. Proximal consonants can play a role in euphony as well as proximal and identical vowels.

> Voici des fruits, des fleurs, des feuilles et des branches.

This line, too, is dominated by labiodental and bilabial consonants, coming as they do at the beginning of the line and of the four tonic syllables. The stressed proximal consonants play a greater role than the identical *d*'s and close *e*'s since these identical sounds occur only in the atonic and insignificant tool-word *des*, a mere partitive article—a word most languages do without, including French in its earlier stages (there being, for example, only one partitive construction in the four thousand-odd lines of the *Chanson de Roland*). Like Verlaine, Lamartine often exploits proximal as well as identical consonants.

> Et des monts et des mers, et des feux et des vents.
> d M z d M   d F z d V

Again, the identical *d*'s and *e*'s play a subsidiary (here, annunciatory) role in relation not only to the identical *m*'s but also to the proximal *f/v* sequence.

A line like the following, from Henri de Régnier,

> Le soleil entrait dans l'antre des forêts

has several euphonious structures working together: (1) the assonanced tonic vowels; (2) the assonance in nasal-*a* in the middle of the line; (3) two "oscillations,"[6] one consonantal, one vocalic, at the beginning: *l-s-l* and ɛ -ã- ɛ (4) the ʊ - ɛ parallelism in the first and final substantives; (5) finally, and this is what concerns us most here, the repeated *tr-d* creates two proximal oscillations since the *d* and the *t* are related phonemically. The end of the line has another proximal oscillation: e- ʊ- ɛ.

To take into account all proximal consonant groups the stylistician needs to borrow the phonetician's chart.

		Bi-labial	Labio-dental	Dental and Alveolar	Palato-alveolar	Palatal	Velar	Uvular
CONSONANTS	Plosive	p b		t d			k g	
	Nasal	m		n		ɲ		
	Resonants			l				ʀ
	Fricative		f v	s z '	ʃ ʒ			
	Semi-vowels	w ɥ				j (ɥ)	(w)	

If we look again at Racine's line, we note that in addition to interior assonance and interior rhyme there are three groups of proximal consonants, that is, adjacent from an articulatory point of view, and two other groups which are related from a vibratory point of view.

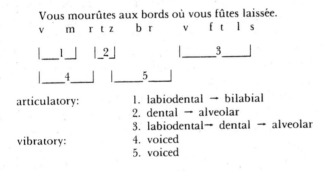

Vous mourûtes aux bords où vous fûtes laissée.

articulatory:
1. labiodental → bilabial
2. dental → alveolar
3. labiodental→ dental → alveolar

vibratory:
4. voiced
5. voiced

Voiced consonants, which the French aptly call *consonnes sonores*, are not only proximal to each other but to all the vowels in the poetic line since all vowels are voiced. Unvoiced consonants have little resonance and contribute to euphony only when participating in other groups. The number of consonants participating in proximal groups here is 9/12 or 75%. The number of voiced consonants is 7/12 or 58%. The number of consonants participating in one or both groups is 100%. This strikingly high percentage surely cannot be irrelevant to the line's oft-vaunted euphony.

Let us now look at a line of Musset deemed euphonious by Grammont to see if the proximity principle still holds.

Les Faunes indolents couchés dans les roseaux

```
l   f   n z  d l     k        d     l   r z
|_1_|_2_| |__3__|          |__4_| |__5_|
        |___6__|               |____7____|
```

articulatory:	1. dental → labiodental
	2. labiodental → dental → alveolar
	3. alveolar → dental
	4. dentals
	5. fricatives (the Parisian R is a fricative as well as a "resonant")
vibratory:	6. voiced
	7. voiced

percentage of proximal consonants: 83%
percentage of voiced consonants: 75%

To discount the impressively numerous patterns of proximal and voiced consonants would minimize unduly the line's full euphonic value (and Musset's good ear). I am ready at this point to posit categorically that a large number of proximal or of "sonorous" consonants within the same line contribute to euphony. If both percentages are high, say 70-80%, a line could be fairly euphonious even without much help from the vowels. The vowels do play the more crucial role, as I shall demonstrate later. But I must insist again that consonants can play—and usually do play— a significant role as well: they are part of a cohesive and highly visible (or better: audible) partnership—they are *not* silent partners—formed to achieve a common goal: euphony.

I have analyzed the 21 lines of Musset specifically mentioned as melodious by Valentine Brunet and the 81 examples of euphony that Grammont takes from Musset and have found the following:

I. from Brunet

percentage of lines having a good number of proximal consonants:

57% of the 21 lines have over 70% proximal consonants
76%   60%

percentage of lines having a good number of voiced consonants:

67% of the 21 lines have over 60% voiced consonants

II. from Grammont

percentage of lines having a good number of proximal consonants:

60% of the 81 lines have over 70% proximal consonants
72%   60%

percentage of lines having a good number of voiced consonants:

58% of the 81 lines have over 60% voiced consonants

We can say with reasonable certainty that these proximal and voiced consonants do contribute to the euphony of these lines since the correlation between lines deemed euphonious by the two critics and the high percentage of these consonants is consistent. The certainty increases with those lines where the percentage is close to (or above) 80%.

*
* *

III. PROGRESSION. By progression is meant the "melodious" flow of vowels and of consonants solely and strictly as they succeed each other in the poetic line with no allowance for gaps or for the overlapping of groups permitted earlier.

Perhaps the safest approach initially would be a negative one: a euphonious progression would be one characterized by an absence of certain dissonant sequences such as the following ones established by J. Marouzeau (*Précis de stylistique française*):

1. overuse of the same vowel in a short interval, especially when accompanied by the same consonant.

Le rat fut à son pied par la patte attaché
        a   a   a   a a
(La Fontaine)
C'est la grande Nounou où nous nous aimerons.
        u   u   u   u   u
(Laforgue)

Musset, through occasional negligence, will be guilty of this type of cacophony:

Sin*on* qu'*on* *en* *en*tend la cloche.

or use it intentionally as a comic device:

Et qu'il est pour*ant temps*, comme dit la chanson.

2. a multiplicity of open syllables in succession, as Musset does deliberately here:

vit d'i-na-ni-tion

3. hiatus, for poetry at least. The romantic poets' deliberate abuse of hiatus is well known and has been parodied:

Où, ô Hugo, huchera-t-on ton nom?
(Laforgue)

4. overuse of certain consonants and consonantal clusters. To Marouzeau's list of harsh consonants should be added the Parisian R when preceded by another consonant and followed by a pause, thus becoming unvoiced: *maître, propre, exècre*. Even one repetition of posterior, uvular R with a frontal vowel such as [i] [y] or the semi-vowel [ɥ] (e.g., *cri, cru, bruit*) could create dissonance in a short poetic line.

5. a high frequency of sibilants, which shocks the French ear even more than that of an Anglophone, the English language being burdened by a plethora of sibilants according to many people who should know: critics, translators, foreigners and especially English poets. One thinks of Tennyson's attempts to rid his verse of sibilants or, as he himself put it, "kicking the geese out of the boat." Poe deliberately invests "The Valley of Unrest" with a high frequency of sibilants to produce an effect of, appropriately enough, unrest. When a French writer like Racine indulges in sigmatism, as in his famous line

Pour qui sont ces serpents qui sifflent sur vos têtes

it is immediately felt by a native ear as deliberate (being used here of course for onomatopoeia). Musset will use sibilants to achieve the same effect:

Quel serpent écrasé s'est dressé sous ses pas?

Poets consciously striving for euphony know even unconsciously that plosive consonants, especially when coming second or third in a cluster, should be well spaced or buffered by softer sounds. The harshness of unvoiced plosives is not simply a subjective notion but scientific fact. Extensive analyses in the field of experimental phonetics using the tape recorder and the oscilloscope reveal the following: "Le tracé des enregistrements nous montre à l'evidence que, dans les plosives, *p, t, k*, on passe sans transition *du silence absolu au bruit le plus violent*: la cassure de la ligne, le saut de l'aiguille enregistreuse ou du spot à l'écran de l'oscilloscope, tout cela confirme l'impression de brusquerie, de choc, de rupture produite par ces phonèmes: là, élasticité zéro. On se heurte à du roc" (H. Morier, *Dictionnaire de poétique*, p. 249). Lucien Rudrauf stresses the "obstructive" nature of unvoiced plosives in relation to the vowels around them: "Les occlusives sourdes, dont l'élasticité et la perméabilité sont nulles, semblent, par leur nature, inaptes à la fonction de transmission. Placée entre deux voyelles sensiblement égales par l'intensité d'accent, l'occlusive sourde se dresse comme un obstacle à franchir. C'est l'affaire d'un instant pendant lequel l'émission vocale cesse, tandis que l'obstacle heurté au passage tend un bruit sec. Si cette image est juste, le rôle de la consonne est purement passif, retardateur, obstructif du circuit dynamique" ("Structure consonantique," p. 14).

Rudrauf has devised a system of stenographic transcription that allows the stylistician to plot the progression of consonants in a poetic line and even in a whole poem. The system has been refined somewhat by Henri Morier as follows:

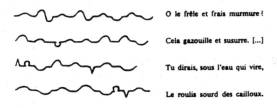

Thus the spirants, liquids, voiced plosives and voiced Parisian R have rounded contours, whereas the harsher sounds—the unvoiced plosives and unvoiced Parisian R—are characterized by angular and jagged lines.[7] Verses like the following, from Verlaine's "Ariettes oubliées," would be charted as follows:

O le frêle et frais murmure !

Cela gazouille et susurre. [...]

Tu dirais, sous l'eau qui vire,

Le roulis sourd des cailloux.

The Rudrauf-Morier system illustrates most graphically the soft, rounded consonantal texture of Verlaine's "La bonne chanson" in which only seven of the fifty-five consonants employed, or less than 13%, are unvoiced plosives and even these are buffered by softer sounds.

La lune blanche

Luit dans les bois ;

De chaque branche

Part une voix

Sous la ramée...

O bien-aimée.

L'étang reflète,

Profond miroir,

La silhouette

Du saule noir

Où le vent pleure...

Rêvons, c'est l'heure.

A positive correlate to the negative principles listed above would be a "principle of maximum ease," or "modulation" (in Frohock's sense), or, as I am suggesting, "progression." The problem with the term "modulation" is that in one of its senses it is a synonym of "euphony" (cf. "the harmonious use of language" in the *American Heritage Dictionary*). However the phenomenon is eventually termed, the analyst can measure the kind of movements the tongue must make to get through the poetic line, the widely held presumption being, once again, that there is a positive correlation between lingual ease and aural pleasure. The examples we will now examine tend to corroborate the presumption.

Thus far I have invoked somewhat aprioristically the principle of progression viewed negatively as an absence of dissonant combinations and positively as orderly or gradual sequence. We can now test this working hypothesis by examining some lines deemed euphonious by a consensus of critics to see if there really is a positive correlation. If so, the principle would seem to have validity.

In testing for euphonious progressions I use three charts and look for the following:

1. a high percentage of proximal vowels as the line progresses so that there are few "maximal leaps" from close to open vowels and from front to back vowels.

2. a low percentage of harsh consonants and the buffering of harsh consonantal clusters. This is made very visible by the use of the Morier-Rudrauf system of consonant transcription, which I have simplified by reducing it to two symbols: rounded ($\cap$) and angular ($\wedge$).

Here we need the full phonetic chart.

		Bi-labial	Labio-dental	Dental and Alveolar	Palato-alveolar	Palatal	Velar	Uvular
CONSONANTS	Plosive	p b		t d			k g	
	Nasal	m		n		ɲ		
	Resonants			l				R
	Fricative		f v	s z '	ʃ ʒ			
	Semi-vowels	w ɥ				j (ɥ)	(w)	
VOWELS						Front	Central	Back
	Close					i y		u
	Half-close					e ø	ə	o ō
	Half-open					ɛ ɛ̃	oe ōœ̃	ɔ
	Open					a		ɑ ɑ̃

First let me analyze the line of French poetry most often cited for its euphony.

EUPHONIC PROGRESSION ANALYSIS

Vous mourûtes aux bords où vous fûtes laissée

I. VOWEL PROGRESSION CHART: APERTURE

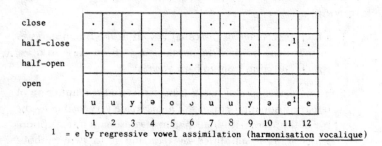

	1	2	3	4	5	6	7	8	9	10	11	12
close	•	•	•				•	•				
half-close				•	•				•	•	•[1]	•
half-open					•							
open												
	u	u	y	ə	o	ɔ	u	u	y	ə	e[1]	e

[1] = e by regressive vowel assimilation (<u>harmonisation</u> <u>vocalique</u>)

II. VOWEL PROGRESSION CHART: ARTICULATION

	1	2	3	4	5	6	7	8	9	10	11	12
front			•					•		•	•	
central				•					•			
back	•	•			•	•	•	•				
	u	u	y	ə	o	ɔ	u	u	y	ə	e	e

III. CONSONANT PROGRESSION CHART: HARSH vs. SOFT

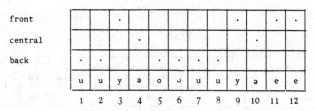

roundness/ angularity	1	2	3	4	5	6	7	8	9	10	11	12	13	14	15	16	17	18
	⌢	⌢	⌣	⋀	⌢	⌢	⌣	⌢	⌢	⋀	⌢	⌢						
	V	M	R	T	Z	B	R	V	F	T	L	S						

Aperture—the only jump comes at the caesura. This is not a maximal leap, and the caesura itself provides buffering. Further buffering is provided by the fact that [o] and [u] are both back vowels.

Articulation—the two maximal leaps are well spaced, and there is not a single vowel that is not followed or preceded by an identical or proximal vowel. Arvède Barine (*Musset*, p. 113), commenting on this line, says that both Racine and Musset know how to exploit the mute *e* to prolong the preceding syllable and give it added resonance. Barine cites the following lines of Musset as examples of the same euphonic strategy.

> Si ce n'est pas ta mère, ô *pâle jeune fille!*

> Quels *mystères* profonds dans l'*humaine* misère!

> *Lentement, doucement*, a côté de Marie.

Consonant progression—there are only two "angular" consonants in the line, and they are not only buffered, they are totally engulfed in softer sounds. Note too that every vowel is preceded or followed by only one consonant. Nine of the twelve consonants, or 75%, are voiced. The phonemic parallelism at the beginning of both hemistiches creates both assonance and interior rhyme.

This, then, is my view of what is happening in Racine's line when we look at it from the point of view of euphony. There is an impressively gradual modulation of vowels, a succession of consonants that have predominately "rounded" contours, high percentages of proximal and voiced consonants as noted earlier, and finally, the most obvious component in context: the end-rhyme.

> Ariane, ma soeur, de quel amour blessée
> Vous mourûtes aux bords où vous fûtes laissée.

In the following lines of Verlaine

> Et je m'en vais
> Au vent mauvais

which are united musically by the rhyme and the four-syllable rhythm, there is not a single vowel higher than *e* and no consonant more posterior than the alveolar [ʒ].

> Et je m'en vais
> Au vent mauvais
> Qui m'emporte
> Deçà, delà
> Pareil à la
> Feuille morte.

In the full stanza there is only one high vowel, [i], and only one large jump: from [i] to nasal, posterior [ã] in the third line. Plosive consonants are few and well spaced, being clustered only in the same third line— a line that perhaps provides needed relief from or contrast to the soft timbre of the general phonemic context.

> Les sanglots longs
> Des violons
>   De l'automne
>
> Blessent mon coeur
> D'une langueur
>   Monotone.

Here, the maximum number of plosives in any line of the stanza is two. The passage is dominated by the soft alliterated *l*'s. There is only one wide jump: between [e] and [ã] in the first line. Whereas Grammont would emphasize the felicitous "modulation" between [e] and [ã], I would again stress the fact that, if such a sequence were repeated frequently at short distance, any euphonic effect achieved by the assonance thus produced would be lessened or even canceled out by the feeling of *effort*.

> Il pleure dans mon coeur
> Comme il pleut sur la ville
> Quelle est cette langueur
> Qui pénètre mon coeur?

Here euphony is assured mainly by the principle of identity: the insistent rhyme scheme imposed upon a short poetic line. But a full account would have to take into consideration the principle of progression. There is only one jerky movement in the stanza: from [y] down to [ã] and back to [i] in line 2. The following line compensates by using a succession of half-open vowels (five out of six), the first three being identical and the only change in the degree of aperture being minimal. The frequency of plosives is as follows: 2:2:2:4. If Verlaine continued the high concentration of plosives of the last line (say, four or five in a six-syllable line), euphony would give way to dissonance, as the reader can test for himself.

*
* *

I have analyzed all 300 lines of Musset (they are all alexandrines) studied by Grammont and my findings are significantly different. In testing for euphonic progression I rated each line on the following objective bases:

score	value	criteria
4	excellent	for vowels: lines having at most one maximal leap from the point of view of aperture and of articulation; for consonants: no clusters of harsh consonants anywhere in the line, i.e., buffering of all harsh consonants
3	good	for vowels: two maximal leaps providing there is buffering between the two leaps; for consonants: one cluster of harsh consonants involving only two phonemes;
2	fair	for vowels: three maximal leaps or two maximal leaps if juxtaposed (i.e., non-buffered); for consonants: a cluster of harsh consonants involving three phonemes;
1	poor	for vowels: 4 maximal leaps for consonants: clusters of harsh consonants involving a total of four or more phonemes within one line;

12	highest possible score for a single line
8-12	good to excellent (5 point spread)
3	lowest possible score for a single line
7-3	fair to poor (five point spread)

Fair to poor lines were given one one additional point if more than 80% of their consonants were proximal and another additional point if more than 80% of their consonants were voiced. Since the cut-off percentage is arbitrary, the standard used is high.

RESULTS:

I. *A la Malibran* (first 100 lines)

percentage of good to excellent lines from the point of view of progression	71%
number of poor to fair lines redeemed by the principle of identity (rhyme *plus* at least one other component e.g., refrain, alliteration, assonance, anaphora, polysyndeton, etc.)	0

number of lines redeemed by a high percentage of proximal and/ or voiced consonants (Juxtaposed unvoiced plosives were not included among the proximal groups)   2

                                                                73%

II.   *Namouna* (first 100 lines)

percentage of good to excellent lines   73%

number of poor to fair lines redeemed by identity   12

number of lines redeemed by proximity (proximal and voiced consonants)   4

                                                                89%

III. *La Nuit de Mai* (first 100 lines)

percentage of good to excellent lines   71%

number of lines redeemed by identity   9

number of lines redeemed by proximity   3

                                                                83%

The average percentage of good lines for all three hundred lines is 81%, which is dramatically higher than Grammont's figure of 38%. The percentage climbs to 84% if we use a less severe cut-off figure of 75% for proximal and voiced consonants in redeeming lines that were rated only "fair" strictly from the point of view of progression.

Even if the "true" percentage (in terms of Absolute, divine Truth) lies somewhere between Grammont's and mine, surely it will be much closer to the higher figure if Musset's poetry is indeed euphonious, as Brunet and dozens of other critics have insisted, and as Grammont himself implies.

When rating lines as "good" or "poor" with regard to euphony, I am not concerned of course with value judgments on the poem itself. Sustained euphony may or may not repulse a hard-boiled reader. A value judgment with regard to euphony will inevitably turn upon an idiosyncratic notion of the correct "dosage." I am concerned neither with the poetic *value* of euphony, nor with special stylistic *effects* that might be achieved through euphony (e.g., an ironic contrast between mellifluous sounds and the "harsh" sense of the general context); I am concerned with its very existence and with objective means of detecting and corroborating that existence. I believe I have developed a valid and efficient method of analysis that can account for the euphony that critics sense but cannot explain in certain poets or certain texts. I make no apology for using quantitative parameters in studying a delicate and slippery subject like euphony. As John Nist has said: "The changing of water either into its components gases or into a solid demonstrates the basic principle about the universe: when differences of DEGREE reach the crucial point, they constitute differences of KIND. All quality, then, is posited upon a CRITICAL QUANTTY. And that quality known as literary style is no exception" ("Ontology of Style," p. 47). Literary critics should not be frightened by false dichotomies or antinomies between the *esprit de géometrie* and the *esprit de finesse*. A good critic often needs both, and often uses one to corroborate the findings of the other. It is not dehumanizing euphony to remove it finally from the already overpopulated realm of the *certain je ne sais quoi*. Wherever there is euphony, there are underlying phonological structures than *can* be objectively analyzed.

PART THREE
Critical Reaction to Musset's Poetry

chapter 9
MUSSET'S POETRY AND
STYLES OF READING

Chapter four was an essay in thematic criticism: I attempted to reach the center of Musset's imaginative world, the core of his consciousness, by examining what I found to be a central and coherent network of frequently recurring images, key words and obsessive themes. To read even a single and short text, as I did in my analysis of Musset's first sonnet in chapter five, with the presumption that it is organized around a theme, matrix or kernel that gives formal unity to the whole is a convention of reading, indeed the chief interpretive strategy of past, present and probably future criticism. It is useful to remember that this convention of unity brackets off, in a kind of Husserlian eidetic reduction, the text's *écarts de soi*, its difference from itself, that is, those strands and warring forces within the text that undermine or subvert its unity, reveal its heterogeneity and transgress the limits the text has set itself, often emphatically, by its overt thematic structure. A deconstructionist reading of Musset would put back those "hidden articulations and fragmentations within assumedly monadic totalities" of which Paul de Man speaks in *Allegories of Reading*. But I submit that before we put back the *écarts*, we first need to establish the *soi*, the text's self-proclaimed identity.

All readings are partial and in both senses of the word. To read is to make choices among a myriad of interpretive moves available to the reader. Each reading and each theory of literature sheds light on certain questions, and the only error, as Jonathan Culler and Wallace Fowlie before him have aptly put it, is to assume that these were the only questions. Despite the uncanny insights of deconstructionist theory and practice, there is no compelling reason why critics cannot go on looking for the major emphases in a text or an opus at the expense of the minor and the marginal. The error, again, would be to think that the major or overt emphasis is all there is to the text or the opus. No post-deconstructionist critic will ever be able to take a text's "unity" for granted, but on the other hand no critic should have to apologize for trying to find it. If not "it," the unity, or even the coherence, then at least the *center*, what the text seems to be trying to say. What it actually does say is of course always more complex and problematical. But focussing on the marginal can happen only in a second moment of literary criticism. The first encounter with the text must be focussed on what it seems to be trying to tell us, its major intention, whether avowed or implicit.

Jonathan Culler has said that what we don't need in literary studies is yet another interpretation of *King Lear*. But Musset's poetic work has been the object of precious few detailed interpretations of the cognitive type, although it has inspired a good deal of criticism of the evaluative type. (Critics have been more prone to judge Musset than to explicate him.) I am going to review the main lines of this evaluative criticism, not to adjudicate between them, but to see by what codes and conventions Musset has been read and judged. If such an approach is the main task of semiotics, as Culler has urged, then, like deconstruction, it can come only as a second moment of criticism and even of a literary history founded, like that of Hans Robert Jauss, on an aesthetics of reception. There will always be a need for practical critics who dare jump in first at the deep end and give us their cogent readings and sincere reactions, whether or not they are conscious of or even care to make explicit the codes and conventions by which they have made sense of what they have read, and there will always be a need for practical critics to provide a text or an opus with a history of reception.

I do not wish what follows to suggest what I call the "conventional fallacy" and what Paul Bové calls a "poetics of coercion"— the idea that the reader has priority and ultimate authority over the text and can, for example, naturalize all newness and strangeness a text may present by simply devising appropriate codes, conventions or other strategies of reading. I am interested here only in the fact that certain codes and conventions do exist (e.g., the reading codes of moralistic criticism, emotional criticism, mimetic criticism, aesthetic criticism, Marxist criticism, feminist criticism, psychocriticism, and the conventions of the lyric) and that some of them work to the advantage, others to the disadvantage of poets like Musset.

*
* *

In his first published volume, *Les Contes d'Espagne et d'Italie*, Musset used words both as mimetic signs and as self-referential signs. The mimetic signs pointed to and described the world outside the text and focussed on a certain area of that world, erotic passion and its often violent consequences. The self-referential signs were used to proclaim a poetry that, already romantic in content, was also self-consciously romantic in style. The readers of 1830 (even the young ones) had been schooled in the neoclassical tradition; they were now brashly challenged to read in a new aesthetic code.

Immediate published reaction to the *Contes* was almost equally divided: eight generally favorable reviews to seven hostile ones.[1] The hostile critics—those writing for *Le Corsaire, La Revue de Paris, Pandore, Gazette de France, Courrier des Théâtres, La Revue Française* and *L'Universel*—were unanimously agreed about the content of the *Contes*. Invoking the conventions of moralistic criticism, they denounced the flattery of vice and debauchery, especially the celebration of extramarital passion, the presumption being, of course, that the reader will be led in the wrong direction, into the path of sin, through the upsetting influence of romantic emotion. Instead of idealizing nature (human nature) the author, they charged, was emphasizing "the ugly."

One example of this moralistic criticism will suffice. Philarète Chasle, writing for the *Revue de Paris* in March 1830, decries in Musset what he calls

> . . . le besoin de développer poétiquement l'individualité humaine, de donner à la versification le plus haut degré de franchise et de liberté possible, de trouver dans la laideur physique et morale une puissance d'émotion inconnue à l'antiquité grecque et romaine; de descendre jusqu'à la peinture des sensations les plus secrètes, des actions les plus vulgaires et de les introduire dans le domaine de l'art, quand même elles seraient basses, ignobles et hideuses.

The passage is interesting in the way it reveals an ultraromantic poet being read through a neoclassical grid or code. First, the distrust of *l'individualité humaine,* as opposed to universal "human nature." Then the shock at seeing traditional canons of taste violated at every turn: in the domain of versification; in the domain of what constitutes a proper object (or subject) for poetry; in the domain of proper (i.e., Graeco-Roman) models; and finally in the domain of seventeenth, eighteenth and early nineteenth-century notions of *bienséance.* Claude Pichois, in a lengthy study of Chasle, has demonstrated that in this influential critic the moralistic code has overwhelmed the code of aesthetic criticism ("La morale écarte sa critique littéraire de l'esthétique" *Philarète Chasle,* p. 494).

The fact that we are dealing here with a convention of reading is evident when one thinks of a quite different reading strategy that could have been used, namely, reading the detailed and enthusiastic description of passion as a healthy catharsis for the reader. The humanistic psychologist Abraham Maslow, for instance, says that the best way of ridding the organism of the lower instincts is to *gratify* them. If they can be gratified vicariously, through literary experiences, so much the better (the opposing convention would read). Or Freud could be invoked and quoted as saying, as he did in his essay on *Wit and its Relation to the Subconscious*, that the reader (like everyone else) has a finite supply of sexual and aggressive energy; when some of that energy is used up, through vicarious experience and emotion, the individual will be less likely to engage in aggressive behavior than one whose supply is still untapped. Comic literature can offer, then, a healthy catharsis. The case for tragic literature had already been cogently argued by Aristotle.

A second proof of the conventionality of moralistic readings of the *Contes* is another move that could be made by a reader favorable to Musset. It is the one made by Maurice Blanchot, who says that in choosing "evil" for his subject a writer reveals man's best way of exercising his freedom. (Freedom, we recall, is the writer's *only* subject according to a neoromantic, Jean-Paul Sartre, who urged, however, that it be used against bourgeois economics more than bourgeois morality.)

The hostile critics also condemned the *Contes* on mimetic and technical grounds. On the mimetic level, they saw exaggeration of passion and violence, *extravagance* and *invraisemblance*. On the technical side they pointed out—using a neoclassical code again—not only the premeditated crimes such as hiatus, enjambement, the use of foreign terms (any use of the latter being judged an abuse), realistic terms (the reviewer writing for *L'Universel* condemned such words as *pots* and *haillons*!) but also unintentional faults such as bad grammar, imperfect rhymes, a lack of coherence in plotting and especially a lack of originality. Seeing the obvious influence of Hugo's *Odes et ballades* and Byron's *Don Juan*, they tried to pass Musset's volume off as the purely derivative work of an adolescent author.

The favorable reviewers—those writing for *Le Globe*, *Le Temps*, *Le Lutin*, *Le Courrier Français*, *Le Nouveau Journal de Paris*, *Le Journal des Débats*, *Le Figaro* and *La Quotidienne*—felt that the "beauties" of the *Contes* outweighed, if they did not outnumber, the main faults. (All fifteen reviewers belonged more or less to a large critical community, *la critique du bon sens*, which condemned the "excesses" of this young disciple of the Cénacle in the name of the Aristotelian golden mean between extremes, that is, the beaten path. The reviewer of *Le Figaro*, for instance, while enthusiastic about Musset's talent, chided him for his "mépris pour les lois du bon sens et de la langue.") The qualities most frequently named were energy, youth, passion, movement, color, verve, naturalness and frankness. Typical of the praise was what the reviewer of *Le Temps* said of *Les Marrons du feu*: "le dialogue est vif, étincelant, passionné, et le rôle de Raphaël est tracé avec un spirituel dévergondage." Another reviewer: "Au fond de tous ces poèmes, on trouvera souvent une création passionnée, une disposition dramatique, de la vie et du mouvement." Musset's dramatic talent was noted by several of the reviewers.

Even the favorable critics were somewhat *déroutés* by the contradictory moods and styles of the *Contes*, their "désordre arrangé," their "sérieux burlesque." The reviewer for *La Quotidienne*, for example, complains about having been "ballottée . . . de la hauteur de la plus belle poésie aux plus incroyables bassesses de langage, des idées les plus gracieuses aux peintures les plus hideuses, de l'expression la plus vive et la plus heureuse aux barbarismes les moins excusables." This type of criticism—like the moralistic criticism—will hound Musset throughout his career. Several critics were puzzled by a poet who seemed to be enthusiastically imitating and subtly parodying romantic authors (himself included) in the very same piece, sometimes in the very same passage. Today's critic is less surprised by texts engaged in self-deconstruction—this trait is now seen as one of the profound tendencies of romanticism.

The favorable reviewers detected originality in Musset's style despite the influence of Hugo and Byron. They praised the poet's audacity and spontaneity, his wit and verve, and the avoidance of traditional and current clichés. *Le Temps* for example:

> M. de Musset cherche avant tout l'originalité. Bien qu'élevé dans l'école romantique, il ne copie pas le maître, il dédaigne les disciples: fort par lui-même, il veut marcher seul, et l'on voit qu'il tend à quelque création indépendante. Aux endroits où sa verve l'entraîne et où l'émotion le domine, il s'exprime avec une franchise libre de toute métaphore étudiée et de toute image parasite. . . Ses qualités comme ses défauts lui sont personnels.[2]

Alexandre Dumas, years later, corroborated this assessment in more general terms:

> Ces vers avaient une qualité, ils étaient vivants; ce n'était ni du Lamartine, ni de l'Hugo, ni du Vigny; c'était une fleur du même jardin, c'est vrai; un fruit du même verger, c'est vrai encore;

mais une fleur ayant son odeur à elle, un fruit ayant son goût
à lui.

Sainte-Beuve, who followed Musset's poetic career from beginning to
end, found the *Contes* somewhat derivative ("Byron seized him and never
let him go") but authentically charming. *Portia* was unequivocally
admired; *Don Paez* and "La Camargo" (*Les Marrons*) were also singled
out for praise but also roundly criticized for their "style trop bigarré
d'enjambements, de trivialités et d'archaïsmes." (*Portraits contemporains*,
II, p. 186). The *Contes* were promising, they announced a true poet,
he said, an adolescent genius possessed of a precocious knowledge of
human passion and a stylist of "easy grace" (*Causeries*, 13, pp. 364-65).
And much later, benefiting from a quarter century of perspective, Sainte-
Beuve explained Musset's originality within the romanticism of the late
1820's: the poetry of the period had been solemn, lofty, religious, often
pompous, dreamy and sentimental. Musset's merit was to reintroduce
wit, verve and irony into French verse and to mix them with a study
of intense passion (*Portraits contemporains*, II, p. 366.)

The most thorough study of Musset's originality in the *Contes* is that
of Pierre Gastinel. He shows that Musset is distinguished from fellow
romantics by his lack of real interest in nature, local color, exoticism,
minute descriptions and his ambivalence toward rich rhyme. And like
Sainte-Beuve he points out that the poems are original in their avoidance
of romantic melancholy, pessimism and "gravity." Musset's ironic
désinvolture is different from Byron's, says Gastinel, in its lack of bitterness
and pessimism. Nor does Musset share Byron's enthusiasm for political
causes; that, for example, of the combatants in Greece. Mardoche keeps
an aristocratic distance from the fray.

> En politique,
> Son sentiment était très aristocratique.
> Et je dois avouer qu'à consulter son goût,
> Il aimait mieux la Porte et le sultan Mahmoud,
> Que la chrétienne Smyrne, et ce bon peuple hellène
> Dont les flots ont rougi la mer hellespontienne.

Philippe Van Tieghem says this about the originality of the *Contes*:

> Cette utilisation des modes romantiques est faite avec une
> aisance et une maîtrise qui sont déjà une originalité. L'auteur
> tient à laisser entendre qu'il ne croit pas tout à fait à ce qu'il
> raconte; non seulement, dans l'ensemble du volume, il tempère
> le sinistre par le plaisant, mais dans le détail d'un poème, il

> corrige le tragique par la fantaisie humoristique. . . . L'harmo-
> nie dans l'attitude morale qui règne dans un ouvrage semble
> un des besoins les plus naturels de l'esprit; c'était une grande
> révolution que de n'en tenir pas compte.
> (*Musset*, p. 15)

In the introduction to her 1973 edition of the *Contes* Margaret Rees corroborates the positive assessment of Musset's originality and stresses the volume's qualities: its technical virtuosity, its relative restraint with regard to exotic detail, its memorable scenes, its fresh imagery, its sense of humor. As an instance of the romantic avant-garde, she says, it is the equivalent of *Hernani* in the theater. My own view is that while it naturally had less impact than Hugo's play (Hugo being a *chef d'école* and Musset a neophyte), it is now a more interesting specimen since, unlike *Hernani*, it is more than a period piece. It is probably the more successful of the two works because it is a less ambitious genre.

*
* *

The publication of the first "livraison" of *Un Spectacle dans un fauteuil*, containing *La Coupe et les Lèvres*, *A quoi rêvent les jeunes filles* and *Namouna*, was the object of a conspiracy of silence on the part of a number of periodicals. Musset was not forgiven by the critics for having poked fun at them in *Les secrètes pensées de Rafaël*. Another problem was the novelty of the genres: *La Coupe* is the first dramatic poem in French literature; *A quoi rêvent* is the first *comédie de fantaisie* in the Shakespearean manner; and *Namouna* is the first extended example of romantic irony by a French poet.

As Arvède Barine points out (*Musset*, pp. 49-50), none of the three poems was accessible to the general public without the aid of extensive commentary. Even the sophisticated members of the Cénacle who listened to Musset's reading of the three works greeted them with deadly silence. Only Mérimée had some kind words to say, and only about *A quoi rêvent*. Still another problem was the confusing plot of *La Coupe* and of *Namouna* and the implausible plot of *A quoi rêvent*. Victor Giraud, writing for the *Revue des deux mondes* in 1936, states the problem thus: "[*Le Spectacle dans un fauteuil*] dont l'inspiration parfois bien incohérente se brisait à chaque instant et se perdait en d'interminables digressions, et qui enfin, à travers toutes sortes d'affectations, de poussées déclamatoires, n'arrivait pas à dégager nettement une pensée maîtresse, un sentiment dominateur, l'unité d'une âme en pleine possession de ses ressources intérieures" ("Le Centenaire des Nuits," p. 456).

Unfavorable reviews (Le Charivari, La Gazette de France, Le Journal des débats, L'Artiste, La France Littéraire) labeled the volume an "indigeste fatras," an "oeuvre sans nom," or spoke of its "fatigantes divagations" (Barine, p. 48); the volume was condemned as "une contrefaçon adroite de lord Byron" and the heroes were condemned for their atheism (P. Siegel, MRG, pp. 4-6). "Le dévergondage, voilà sa poétique," said the reviewer of the Débats. The reviewer, who signed the article as "J.S.," labeled Musset a mediocre poet and his poetry "une poésie de roué." The critic's objectivity can be questioned since the J.S. was none other than Jules Sandeau, whom Musset had supplanted as George Sand's lover. Years later, writing in June 1841, for La Presse, Sandeau will rectify his vituperative judgment and call Musset "l'esprit le plus fin, le plus varié, le plus exquis et le plus charmant de l'époque" (quoted by M. Allem, Musset, p. 69). Even a friendly critic, Ulric Guttinguer, a recent convert to Catholicism, was saddened, he said in the Revue de Rouen, by the "dérèglement d'un coeur incrédule où aucune pensée principale ne domine" (Quoted by Allem, p. 70).

On the other hand five reviews (La Revue de Paris, La Revue Encyclopédique, Le Temps, La Quotidienne and La Revue des Deux Mondes) were impressed with Musset's talent, verve and originality. The reviewer of Le Temps compared Musset's talent favorably with Lamartine's. Then, reading Un Spectacle strictly through the code of aesthetic criticism, he suggests that on the level of the work's purely formal qualities, he places Musset ahead of Vigny and even Hugo: "Si la poésie résidait tout entière dans la forme, j'avoue qu'à n'écouter que mon sentiment personnel, je n'hésiterais pas à placer M. de Musset à la tête de tous les poètes sans exception que la France a vu surgir depuis quinze ans" (Allem, ibid.). Sainte-Beuve proclaimed that the Spectacle "classe définitivement son auteur parmi les plus vigoureux artistes de son temps" (RDM, janvier, 1833). And Mlle Clémence Robert, writing for the Journal des Femmes in 1834, states that Musset writes for an intellectual élite interested in the development of the imagination (Siegel, MRG, p. 8).

*
* *

It is Musset's extended lyrics that have received the most critical attention. Again, critics have focused on affective more than cognitive issues and have judged Musset more than they have explicated him. This is fitting in a way since Musset's poetry is less richly ambiguous than that of other poets. He attempted a direct, spontaneous lyricism rather than the transposition of an emotional experience into recondite symbolism or complex objective correlatives requiring ingenious interpretations. The affective issue is really an aesthetic one, it questions the very validity of a poetic genre that allows a poet to sing so directly of himself.

Negative readings of Musset's lyrics were the natural result of poetic texts being filtered through hostile aesthetic codes. Advocates of the late romantic concept of *art utile* (e.g., Hugo in *William Shakespeare* and Lamartine in *Cours familier de littérature*) considered Musset's lyrics as inconsequential, puerile and "soft." Partisans of art for art's sake and the Parnassians, especially Leconte de Lisle and Catulle-Mendès, will class Musset among the *montreurs*, the emotional exhibitionists, and condemn his lax versification. Baudelaire places Musset in the *école mélancolico-farceuse*, condemning a poetry that rejects craftsmanship in favor of facile inspiration. Rimbaud (in the *lettre du voyant* of 1871) will complain: "Musset est quatorze fois plus exécrable pour nous, générations douloureuses et prises de visions, que sa paresse d'ange a insultées." When Verlaine shouts

> Prends l'éloquence et tords-lui son cou!

it is Musset's neck, among others, he is after. Moralistic criticism e.g., Veuillot, Hello, Sully-Prudhomme, Swinburne (who thought Musset indolent, self-indulgent, effeminate, callous and prurient) and many Catholic critics will condemn the dangerous unwholesomeness of the love lyrics while praising other aspects of the opus. (Many Catholic critics appreciated *L'Espoir en Dieu*, the *Lettre à M. de Lamartine* and two edifying passages of *Rolla* that express nostalgia for a lost faith.) Decadents, symbolists and later most of the surrealists (Musset is not even mentioned in Eluard's anthology of nineteenth century poetry) will condemn the banality of theme and the declamatory grandiloquence of the *Night* cycle. Henri Guillemain expresses the last complaint thus: "La douleur vraie, la souffrance, pas littéraire, la souffrance-souffrance, elle n'est pas éloquente" ("Notes sur Musset," p. 468).

The large anti-romantic movement of the twentieth century—the attack was led by Gide, Charles Maurras, Léon Daudet, Pierre Lasserre, Henri Massis, Julien Benda, and the editorial staff of the *Nouvelle Revue*

Française—will condemn the anti-rationalist impulse in poets like Musset, the self-pitying and lachrymose melancholy and a sentimentality that is judged self-indulgent, melodramatic and frivolous.

Musset's lyrics will likewise be condemned as a blatant *étalage du moi* by those espousing an aesthetic based on impersonality in art and who criticize the poet for not placing adequate aesthetic distance between the original experience and its artistic elaboration. Flaubert offers the following summary of Musset's entire opus:

> Musset a eu de beaux jets, de beaux cris, voilà tout. . . . Les nerfs, le magnétisme, voilà sa poésie L'esthétique du sentiment est la ruine de l'art.
> (Letter to Louise Colet, 30 May 1852)

> Personne n'a fait de plus beaux fragments que Musset, mais rien que des fragments, pas une oeuvre! Son inspiration est toujours trop personnelle. . . Charmant poète, d'accord; mais pas grand, non!
> (Letter to Louise Colet, 23 September 1852)

Croce and Valéry will hang Musset by the same rope. Croce was not convinced that Musset's lyrical poetry was true poetry because it did not offer an objectification of the poet's passions; he preferred Musset's theater, which converts the writer's "heart" from subject to object, that is, an objet d'art (see S. Jeune, *FL*, pp. 85-86).

Predictably, Marxist critics, with the notable exception of Aragon, have treated Musset's poetry with benign neglect in favor of his dramaturgy; the latter reflects the decadence of modern bourgeois society and can thus be reconciled with socialist realism and even a *littérature engagée*. Henri Lefèbvre, the best of Musset's Marxist critics, dismisses Musset's poetry as that of an uninventive rhetorician and as an apprenticeship for his real calling, the theater. (As early as 1847 two critics, Alexandre Dufaï and Armand de Pontmartin, criticized Musset for not using his prodigious talent as an ironist and satirist against social and political evils.)

Lamartine sums up the negative criticism as well as anyone:

> Enfant aux blonds cheveux, jeune homme au coeur de cire,
> Dont la lèvre a le pli des larmes ou du rire,
> Selon que la beauté qui règne sur tes yeux
> Eut un regard hier sévère ou gracieux;
> Poétique jouet de molle poésie,
> Qui prend pour passion ta vague fantaisie,
> Bulle d'air coloré dans une bulle d'eau
> Que l'enfant fait jaillir du bout d'un chalumeau. . .

Honte à qui croit ainsi jouer avec sa lyre!
La vie est un mystère et non pas un délire.
    ("A M. de Musset, en réponse à ses vers")

> L'absence de ces trois qualités [un pur amour, une foi, un caractère] donne à l'ensemble des oeuvres de Musset quelque chose de vide, de creux, de léger dans la main, d'incohérent, de sardonique, d'éternellement jeune, et par conséquent de souvent puérile et de parfois licencieux qui ne satisfait pas la raison. . . une influence maladive et funeste. . . . Cette poésie est un perpétuel lendemain de fête, après lequel on éprouve cette lourdeur de tête. . . . Poésie de la paresse, et cet alanguissement de vie qu'on éprouve le matin à son réveil après une nuit de festin, de danse et d'étourdissement de liqueurs malsaines qu'on a savourées. . . . Philosophie du plaisir, qui n'a pour moralité que le déboire et le dégoût.
>   (*Cours familier*, 18e entretien, 1857)

Lamartine thus castigates Musset with a Beuvian-like "formula:" if Chateaubriand for Sainte-Beuve was a "Catholique à l'imagination épicurienne," Musset for Lamartine is a *puer senex* refusing to mature and whose poetry is a perpetual hangover. The formula neatly covers the reading codes used by moralistic and aesthetic critics, purists and utilitarians alike.

*
* *

The indictment of Musset's lyrical poetry is thus lengthy and detailed. It is indicted not only on many different counts but from widely different points of view. However, witnesses for the defense have not been hesitant in coming forth.

Sainte-Beuve, whose jealousy of Musset was more than tempered by his honesty and by his critical acumen, offered in the final analysis a balanced judgment. Musset was overrated, he said, he never lived up fully to his promise, he wasted his gifts, behind his verse there was the smell of what Lamartine called a hangover and what Sainte-Beuve himself calls a "saoulerie;" nevertheless he was impressed by what he considered Musset's best efforts. *Souvenir* was judged "d'une émouvante et pure beauté" (*Causeries*, XIII, p. 370). And the "*Nuit de Mai* restera un des plus touchants et des plus sublimes cris d'un jeune coeur qui déborde, un des plus beaux témoignages de la moderne Muse" (*Portraits contemporains*, II, p. 218). In fact all the *Nuits* were deemed "immortal" as were *Rolla* and the one lyrical canto, the second, of *Namouna* ("les

deux cents vers les mieux lancés et les plus osés que la poésie française
se fût jamais permis" *Causeries*, XIII, p. 367).

Sainte-Beuve was not alone in this sort of praise. Both Heine and Taine
called Musset France's greatest lyric poet. Brunetière, Faguet, Lemaître,
Brandeis and Zola hailed him as "the most" touching, moving, human,
sincere of the romantic poets. There is a mimetic code involved here:
vérité d'émotion (a term used by Faguet and Brunetière). Emile Montégut,
for instance, says of *Souvenir*: "C'est le sentiment pur, nu comme la
vérité, lorsqu'elle s'échappe hors de son puits, avant aucun revêtement,
sans apprêt et presque sans souci de l'art, un jet de passion, sorti tout
chaud du coeur" (*Nos Morts*, p. 298). This judgment is repeated in the
mid twentieth century by that most lucid of Musset's critics, Philippe
Van Tieghem.

> L'habitude de ne composer que dans des moments de tension
> nerveuse n'influe pas seulement sur la forme extérieure du
> poème; elle entraîne certains caractères dans le contenu même
> de l'oeuvre. Ne doit-on pas s'expliquer par là cette impression
> que font nos autres lyriques en comparaison de Musset, et même
> dans leurs poèmes les plus sincères, d'être singulièrement sereins
> et comme extérieurs à leurs emotions? N'est-il pas vrai que chez
> Hugo la plus incontestable des douleurs semble, dans quelque
> *A Villequier*, devenir un prétexte à belle ordonnance oratoire?
> Et Musset n'est-il pas le seul à conserver brûlante encore
> l'émotion qui lui a mis la main à la plume? (*Musset*), p. 35)

In 1923 Croce wondered whether Musset was an authentic poet; in 1957
Philippe Soupault asserted that he was indeed and invited future scholars
to take Musset's poetry less lightly than past scholars and fellow poets
had done.

It is interesting to note that where some critics have found weakness,
others have found strength; Zola, Faguet and Barbey spoke of the "power"
of Musset's sensibility, for instance. Even more interesting is the fact
that where some have decried the purely personal nature of Musset's lyrics,
others have seen their universality. Barbey said of Musset that he was
the "fullest representative of us all in fact who has. . . ever existed (quoted
by M. Rees, *Musset*, p. 3). The superlative is suspect, but the praise has
been repeated by others. By Taine for example: "Y eut-il jamais accent
plus vibrant et plus vrai? Celui-là au moins n'a jamais menti. . . . Il a
fait la confession de tout le monde. . . . Chacun retrouvait en lui ses
propres sentiments, les plus fugitifs, les plus intimes. . . Alors ont éclaté
ces sanglots dans tous les coeurs" (quoted by S. Jeune, *FL*, p. 138). Seeing

it as representative of modern man, both Gilbert Ganne and Antoine Adam have spoken of Musset's romanticism as "our" romanticism. Ganne, explaining why Musset is still alive in the second half of the twentieth century says this: "La détresse et les plaintes de Musset, chacun de nous peut s'y reconnaître, dans ces régions secrètes où nul ne peut se mentir: c'est la détresse et les plaintes de l'enfant blessé et déçu" ("Sa jeunesse," p. 76.). Antoine Adam, in an article entitled "Son romantisme est le nôtre," offers the following explanation of Musset's continuing relevance.

> Ceux-là se trompent qui lui reprochent un fade sentimentalisme. Si dans son oeuvre la passion s'exprime avec de tels excès, c'est qu'une vie tout entière vouée à l'amour et dévorée par lui représente le mieux l'absolu dans une existence d'homme. . . .
>
> Il y avait chez Musset cette horreur de la vie et cette extase de la vie que Baudelaire observait en lui-même. . . .
>
> Ce qu'il découvrait en s'éloignant de ses premiers amis, c'était cette poésie de l'inquiétude et des déchirements tragiques, cette poésie de l'homme moderne que le véritable romantisme avait suscité, c'était cette vision d'un monde merveilleux et vivant que l'esprit du poète romantique évoque par les miracles de la fantaisie.
>
> Ce romantisme-là, c'est le nôtre. C'est lui qui se retrouve au fond de l'inquiétude de notre siècle, et les mêmes problèmes qui hantaient la jeunesse de 1830 continuent de solliciter notre génération.
>
> (*Les Nouvelles Littéraires*, 9 mai 1957, p. 4)

*

* *

The favorable response to Musset's most personal lyrics can be explained by several closely related codes and conventions that work in his favor.

1. There is a "biographical convention" (Culler, *Structuralist Poetics*, p. 178) that tells the reader to make a poem significant by discovering in it signs of a passion, thought or reaction, and then by reading it as a gesture whose significance lies in the context of a life. Directly related to the biographical convention are various forms of psychological and phenomenological criticism in which *all* literary language is read as "gestural" and therefore expressive of the author's experiential stance (the self-world relationship), his motives and moods, his character, in short his entire consciousness, or, for neo-Freudian "psychocritiques," his unconscious. Since stylistic patterns and experiential patterns are not isomophic, the danger of such approaches is that they can lead to what

I have called elsewhere (*In Search of Style*, p. 5) the "intentionality fallacy." But most of the conclusions of psychological criticism have been correct because the evidence (including extra-literary sources) is overwhelming— as is the case with Musset—and not because of a *necessary* connection between stylistic patterns in an opus and the author's psyche. Since in his lyrical poetry at least Musset is an exemplary romantic, there is a close correlation between the mythical author (i.e., the sum of his poetic personae, what phenomenologists call *l'homme de Musset* and *l'être mussétien*) and the empirical, historical author of flesh and blood—this was indeed the whole point of poetry for Musset.

Critics reading within the biographical convention will explicate and judge Musset's poetry by looking for the relationships between *l'expérience écrite* and *l'expérience vécue*. Gustave Lanson for instance will say of Musset that he lived his poetry, that it is the diary of his life; Paul Stapfer will say that it is impossible to separate the author from the man: "to read his poetry is to read his life" (*Musset*, p. 6); Robert Denommé will entitle an essay: "Musset and the Poetry of Experience;" and Emile Henriot will say: "Pas un mot, chez lui, pas un vers que la réalité n'ait dictée, que n'anime une émotion qui n'ait été vraiment éprouvée, ressentie" (*Musset*, p. 185)

2. The code of emotional criticism ties literary excellence to emotional power. A dogmatic romantic version of the code is that poetry *must* be personal in origin and must aim at the production of a like emotion in the reader. Musset's very poetics and praxis are based on this code, and therefore it comes as no surprise that his work will please those readers who share the same conviction. Some examples of this type of reading:

> Comme tout part du coeur et comme tout va au coeur!
> (P. Stapfer, *Musset*, p. 18)
> Les raisons de la permanence de Musset:. . . . En premier lieu, c'est le langage du coeur. . . Si le langage du coeur, marqué de spontanéité, de fraîcheur et d'abandon, s'allie aux prestiges de l'esprit, il a des chances d'atteindre au chef-d'oeuvre.
> (Gilbert Ganne, "Sa jeunesse," p. 76)
> L'art n'est pas d'arranger des mots, mais d'exprimer des passions: il s'agit d'émouvoir et non d'épater.
> (Albert Allenet, quoted by P. Siegel, *MRG*, p. 84)
> Musset réveillera dans les coeurs les exaltations sentimentales dont le romantisme nous a rendu la fierté, et, par lui, quiconque aura aimé et pleuré s'en croira plus grand.
> (Albert Pauphilet, quoted by S. Jeune *FL*, p. 81)

3. There is a more general convention of reading poetry, which Culler calls "the rule of significance," the code by which all poetry, whether personal or impersonal, must be read as presenting an idiosyncratic attitude or philosophical stance, at least by implication, with regard to a problem concerning mankind in general and not just the poet in particular.

Many critics, among them Paul Bourget, Zola and Anatole France, have praised Musset for his *humanité*. For Paul Alexis this is the single most important criterion for determining an author's greatness (see *MRG*, p. 89). Musset is likewise seen by many critics as representative of his period, of his century, of modern man's metaphysical anguish and pessimism, and by others as the incarnation of eternal youth. Zola: "D'où vient donc l'étrange puissance de Musset sur sa génération? C'est qu'il a jeté le cri de désespérance du siècle, c'est qu'il a été le plus jeune et le plus saignant de nous." (*Nouveaux Contes à Ninon*, p. 166). "Musset est plus humain que tous les poètes de son temps," asserts André Claveau (*Musset*, p. 207); this assertion is in fact part of the conventional wisdom regarding French romanticism.

The "rule of significance" confers "depth" to the (presumed) experience related by the lyric poet. As Veronica Forrest-Thomson explains in her "Levels of Poet Convention:" "Poetic language stands for a state of being imaginatively aroused, hence for depth of experience" (p. 41). Thus critics like Maurice Donnay will praise Musset for presenting deep emotions *sub specie aeternitatis*: "Ici l'individualisme se fond dans l'humanité; un tel poème éveille en chacun de nous les échos des émotions profondes: il les fixe, ces émotions, 'sous l'aspect de l'éternité'. Voilà pourquoi il n'y a rien, dans notre langue, qui soit supérieur aux *Nuits*" (*Musset*, pp. 131-32).

4. The rule of significance leads naturally or logically to the "convention of impersonality." Culler explains: "Even in poems which are ostensibly presented as personal statements made on particular occasions, the conventions of reading enable us to avoid considering that framework as a purely biographical matter" (*Structuralist Poetics*, p. 167). As the theme develops, the reader not only gives it an increasingly universal application but places it more and more in an atemporal framework. As René Wellek, Cleanth Brooks and others have pointed out, the "I" of a lyrical poem is dramatic. This dramatic speaker or persona is a guarantor, really, of impersonality. Both T. S. Eliot and I. A. Richards have expatiated on the objectification of emotion in the poetic artifact:

there is no one-to-one relation between the poet's original emotion and the emotion of the poem he creates. What is produced, says Eliot, is not the repetition of an earlier emotion but a new thing resulting from the concentration or distillation of a great number of experiences; poetry is not a turning loose of emotion, but an escape from emotion; it is not the expression of personality, but an escape from personality.

Many of Musset's critics have noted that the former mistress evoked by a singular noun or pronoun in the *Night* cycle and elsewhere is really a composite of all the important women in the poet's love life. And the emotion presented in any passage of his longer lyrics is a distillation of many experiences happening at different times in his life and subtly different in kind.

Even if all this were not true (but it is), readers tend to read this way *anyway*. A powerful convention almost forces the reader to seek the general in the particular.

5. The "convention of monumentality" allows the reader to make of even the most impassioned lyric more than the mere development of an exclamation, a simple *cri de coeur*. The very hardness of the medium—

> Sculpte, lime, cisèle

—produces in the reader of poetry an expectation that he is dealing with something more durable than bronze.

> Exegi monumentum aere perennius.

Horace was right after all. His poetry *has* outlived most of the metal monuments of ancient Rome. Milton too was right:

> What needs my Shakespeare for his honored bones
> The labor of an age in pilèd stones?
>
> . . .
>
> Thou in our wonder and astonishment
> Hast built thyself a livelong monument.

Even a short poem like a sonnet, says Ronsard, can monumentalize and immortalize his beloved Hélène. Indeed with a classic of world literature the convention of monumentality expands into an expectation of earthly immortality, what Malraux called an *anti-destin*. (Zola will praise Musset's *cris de coeurs*, speaking of "l'immortalité de ses sanglots.") And even with poems that are not literary *monuments classifiés* the strength of the convention is so strong that even the prosaic lines of a Jacques Prévert, for instance, take on a certain monumentality.

> Il a mis le café
> Dans la tasse
> Il a mis le lait
> Dans la tasse de café
> Il a mis le sucre
> Dans le café au lait
> Avec la petite cuiller
> Il a tourné
> Il a bu le café au lait
> Et il a reposé la tasse
> Sans me parler

The typographical disposition and the "imposing margins of silence" (Culler) induce a "poetic attitude" (Genette, Rosengren, Baumgärtner) in the reader who then processes the text in such a way that the trivial becomes exemplary and a moment of epiphany.

6. Then there are the conventions which allow the reader to inscribe a poem in a poetic tradition or genre, those for instance of the extended lyric in general and of the greater Romantic lyric in particular. Such conventions transform the deictics that anchor the text to a specific situation of utterance to a level of discourse that involves the general human condition (*Structuralist Poetics*, pp. 165-67.). That is, the conventions of the lyric reinforce "code 3," the rule of significance. The deictics provide a point of departure, used first in the service of concreteness—a concrete underpinning, if you will, to the thoughts and feelings of a meditative persona. The meditations in *The Eolian Harp*, *Tintern Abbey*, *Le Lac*, *Tristesse d'Olympio* and Musset's *Souvenir* move (as meditations usually do) from the particular to the general. At the end of a typical greater Romantic lyric the poem returns to its deictics, anchoring itself once again to its specific situation of discourse, in the interests both of concreteness and of verisimilitude. But the reader by now has been caught up in the universal import of the developing theme and subsumes the particular under the general.

Another convention of the extended lyric is the expectation of loftiness of theme and diction (e.g., the "embarrassing" device of apostrophe in the greater Romantic lyric). The register is that of the sublime, which elevates the theme above empirical contexts and asserts the poem's impersonal monumentality (see *Structuralist Poetics*, p. 187). Longinus asserted that the purpose of the sublime register was not only to persuade but to "take the reader out of himself." The sublime usually takes the poet too out of himself as he gets more and more caught up in the argument and less and less in his autobiography. Even should the poet assert that he alone has delighted or suffered in this way, the sublime register deconstructs such assertions "upwards," as it were, to a more universal level. Proof of the fact that Musset does not consider his emotional situation unique is the high frequency of maxims in the *Night* cycle.

(Note that the conventions that obtain for the greater Romantic lyric do not obtain for the romantic novel. Musset will have to devote an entire chapter of heavy rhetoric in *Les Confessions d'un enfant du siècle* to convince the reader that the autobiographical hero is indeed an *enfant du siècle*, representative of a group and emblematic of an era.)

7. There are other and more practical conventions for processing poems that could be expressed in the form of rules or imperatives.

—Look for the text's unity; or, failing that,

—Look for "totality" (Culler), coherence, "lyrical consistency" (Jauss); or, failing that,

—Look for the text's center of gravity.

—Look for the text's level of verisimilitude (e.g., realism, the fantastic, the *merveilleux*, the sublime).

—Look for phonemic, lexical and syntactical parallelisms; they will reveal parallelisms of thought.

—Look for binary oppositions, dialectical resolutions of binary oppositions, displacements of unresolved oppositions by a third term, four-term homologies, series united by a common denominator, etc.

Such imperatives tend to work in favor of all poets, good and bad. When we "fail" to find a unifying or plausible structure in a poetic text, we do tend to consider this our failure as readers and not the poet's. It is our obtuseness that has made the text opaque.

Many critics have complained about the incoherence of certain poems and certain passages in Musset's work; many others have taken the unity of these texts (too much?) for granted.

Another practical convention that is particularly helpful to lyric poets like Musset is the imperative that tells the reader to read synecdochally or symbolically whenever possible, that is, whenever plausible. Synecdochally, Musset's Pelican represents the entire species, symbolically all true poets. The very fact that Musset uses the capital P for the Poet of the *Nuits* is an open invitation to the reader to read synecdochally rather than strictly on the level of one man's biography. Reading a poem metonymically, as indirection, displacement or catachresis (Riffaterre), that is, interpreting the poem as saying one thing in terms of another, is more important in post-romantic poetry (in France, after Nerval), but critics of the next two or three centuries may surprise us—and even make us turn over in our graves—by reading Musset more radically than we do now.

8. In texts like *Namouna* in which a long and serious canto is framed by the comic and flippant verve of the first and second cantos, and in which the narrator assumes an ambivalent attitude toward his hero and his story, the modern convention of reading towards irony and paradox gives the poem is "modern appeal." Musset's rapid and contradictory shifts of theme and tone disconcerted many of his contemporaries but pleases many of mine. *Namouna*, says Aragon, is the only poem in French literature that can approach Pushkin's *Eugene Onegin* and is "one of the greatest poems ever written." The surrealist in Aragon admires the poem's capricious fantasy; the Marxist in him admires the refracted reflections of concrete historical and socio-economic conditions; the modern reader in him admires the text's romantic irony. Similarly, Gilbert Ganne finds Musset's modern appeal in his paradoxical temperament: "La seconde raison de la permanence de Musset. . . c'est son tempérament, à la fois léger et profond, impertinent et grave, brillant et tragique, insouciant et douloureux, galant et épris" ("Sa jeunesse," p. 77).

9. Another modern convention of reading is what might be called "the rule of ambiguity," the rule that says that a literary work *must* be read as ambiguous, that a literary work always says more than what the writer meant to say, and often says something quite different from what he thought he said. This convention is especially strong among readers of poetry. William Empson explained it well: the reason poetry is more ambiguous than prose, he said, is that readers of poetry have been trained to expect it. An extreme version of the code was expressed by Valéry: "L'oeuvre dure en tant qu'elle est capable de paraître tout autre que son auteur l'avait faite" (quoted by Wallace Fowlie, *French Critics*, p. 135). Simon Jeune has applied a similar statement of Valéry—"L'oeuvre dure pour s'être transformée"—to Musset's poetry. He documents the fact

that the elegiac and romantic *enfant du siècle* was admired by the first and second generations of Musset's readers and condemned by the anti-romantic school of the early twentieth century; however, alongside the anti-romantics another group of critics were discovering a new and "classical" Musset, a poet who has a taste for general ideas and whose chief and enduring qualities were clarity, simplicity, common sense, taste, tact and *mesure*, psychological penetration, a poet for whom memory and nostalgia were important.[3]

When heavy stress is placed on the difference between what text and author are trying to say and what they actually do say at certain moments, the convention of ambiguity becomes that of deconstruction, which is simply one reading strategy among others. A simple example would be my reading of *L'Espoir en Dieu*, a poem that purports to express a faith but which ends up expressing an anguish. A deconstructionist reading of Musset's *Night* cycle would reveal the impersonal side of the personal poetry; such a reading was attempted briefly in chapter two and again in this chapter, notably in the discussion of certain reading conventions: the rule of significance, the conventions of impersonality and monumentality and of the lyric genre. For those critics fond of "aesthetic distance" such a deconstructionist reading might reveal that Musset was a better poet than he meant to be.

10. Musset's poetry may be seen in still another light by the reader is she employs an entirely different code or style of reading from those enumerated above, and her conclusions can be just as cogent. If the meaning of a work is the experience of a reader, what difference does it make, asks Jonathan Culler, if the reader is a woman? One of the most popular critical clichés of nineteenth-century criticism was that Musset's appeal was especially strong among the young and among women. Today we would have to modify the assertion to read "certain women." What do we know of Musset's appeal to that new entity, "the modern woman?"

Feminist criticism, as Elaine Showalter has explained, is concerned "with the way the hypothesis of a female reader changes our apprehension of a given text, awakening us to the significance of its sexual codes" (quoted by Culler, *On Deconstruction*, p. 50). A female reader can identify of course with the concerns of women characters; but a female reader who is also a feminist can study her own reactions and those of others involved when a woman reader is led to identify with male characters or male personae against her own interests as a woman or in complicity with the interests of the male (ibid., p. 51).

A feminist reading of Musset has not yet been attempted, but some of the interesting questions can be foreseen. First, relations between the sexes, especially as influenced by History. Musset himself dealt with this subject in the second chapter of *La Confession d'un enfant du siècle*. Second, various complexes (Don Juan, Oedipus, Narcissus) and fixations (mother, sister). Third, sexual stereotypes. I touched on this briefly in connection with the *Contes d'Espagne et d'Italie*, but the entire opus could be examined from this point of view. Gobineau, for instance, has complained that the Mussetian woman is always an object of pleasure. The Muse of the *Nuits* is also problematical. Culler offers a brief but suggestive discussion of the problem.

> Discussions of women that appear to promote the feminine over the masculine—there are, of course, traditions of elaborate praise—celebrate the woman as goddess (Venus, Muse, Earth Mother) and invoke a metaphorical woman, in comparison with which actual women will be found wanting. Celebrations of woman or the identification of women with some powerful force or idea—truth as a woman, liberty as a woman, the muses as women—identify actual women as marginal. Women can be a symbol of truth only if one presumes that those seeking truth are men. The identification of woman with poetry through the figure of the muse also assumes that the poet will be a man. While appearing to celebrate the feminine, this model denies women as active role in the system of literary production and bars them from the literary tradition.
>
> (*On Deconstruction*, p. 166)

Musset did put Woman on a precarious pedestal. Listen, for example to George Sand: "Hélas! oui, cet enfant voudrait pour maîtresse quelque chose comme la Vénus de Milo armée du souffle de ma patronne sainte Thérèse" (*Elle et Lui*, chap. 9). Henri Lefèbvre agrees:

> Il veut l'infini dans un être vivant et fini, dans un être faible, et qu'il veut faible et doux. Il veut un corps vierge, et une maîtresse ardente—une soif et un désir analogues aux siens en même temps qu'une présence qui l'apaise. Il exige à la fois l'expérience et la pureté, ce qui vient de l'impudeur et ce qui la nie, la perfection inhumaine et l'humaine féminité. Il demande à sa maîtresse de ne pas lui résister et en même temps de rester pour lui le mystère, l'inaccessible.
>
> (*Musset*, p. 61)

I can well imagine a feminist critic being rather more impatient with Musset than those critics reading within a male reading code. And still more impatient with such critics. Here for instance is one of them.

> La chaudière y semble toujours près d'éclater sous une pression trop forte, et voilà bien ce qui ravit la jeunesse et les femmes toujours disposées aux paroxysmes. Parmi les nombreuses et fidèles admiratrices de Musset, beaucoup doivent avoir, comme lui, la passion de l'instantané et de l'immédiat. Entre leur rêve et la réalité, entre le désir et la possession, elles n'admettent aucun obstacle, aucun retard. Les buts éloignés leur paraissent chimériques. C'est ici et point ailleurs; c'est tout de suite ou jamais. Et Musset lui-même est bien comme elles, impatient de toute opposition et de tout délai, incapable d'attente, esclave de sa passion présente, *impotens cupidinis, impatiens morae.*
>
> La jeunesse et les femmes se reconnaissent et s'adorent en lui. Elles l'aiment plus peut-être pour ses sympathiques défauts que pour ses mérites supérieurs. Il est fait à leur image, et naturellement cette image leur est chère. Elles le trouvent plus vrai que les autres parce qu'il est plus près d'elles et de leur faiblesse, parce qu'il est terriblement femme, lui aussi.
> (André Claveau, *Musset*, pp. 203-04)

Here is a critic using a male reading code with a vengeance and who needs some consciousness-raising. Woman is situated in an essentialistic ontology, frozen ("toujours") in an attitude of impatience and paroxysm, and Musset is made in her image. Pierre Moreau, in much the same vein, has said (in both *Ames romantiques* and *Classicisme des romantiques*) that it is to women that Musset speaks, and that male readers have the impression of intercepting a message.

Other critics speak of Musset's "feminine virtues"—his charm, his delicacy, his refined sensibility; Andre Suarès for example: "le charmant Musset, si fin, si vrai, si femme!" (quoted by S. Jeune, *FL*, p. 153). Once a water-tight definition of the feminine sensibility and of what it means to be a woman has been achieved, perhaps an astute feminist critic may uncover new virtues in our mythical author and a feminist biographer may find analogous ones in the man himself.

APPENDIX
NOTES
BIBLIOGRAPHY
INDEX

appendix
ANOTHER EXAMPLE OF THE
GREATER ROMANTIC LYRIC:

SOUVENIR DES ALPES

Like the more famous *Souvenir*, studied earlier, *Souvenir des Alpes* fulfills the generic requirements of the greater Romantic lyric: (1) an extended poem involving an interaction between a natural setting and the observing subject and modulating into a sustained meditation; (2) a determinate speaker in a particularized setting begins with a description of the landscape, an aspect of which evokes a varied process of memory, thought, anticipation or feeling which remains closely interinvolved with the outer scene; (3) during the course of meditation the lyric speaker either achieves an insight, faces up to a tragic loss, comes to a moral decision or resolves the emotional problem.

*
* *

(1) At the outset the weary, lonely and dejected traveler looks selectively at Nature, seeing at first only signs of impermanence: the golden "dust" of the burning "sand" fluttering (*voltigeait*) before him; a ramshackle ("pauvre") hostelry; an old, worm-eaten bridge; a flowing river; a restive mule; birds in movement singing to each other of love and melancholy. The pathetic fallacy here—a hyperbole of romantic interaction between subject and object—is repeated later with a black eagle "burdened with care."

(2) The determinate speaker, the *voyageur*, is Musset himself returning from Italy through the Alps after the break-up of his affair with George Sand. The particularized setting is the specific mountain relay station where Musset had actually stopped and before which rises a particular summit: le mont Rose.

Two aspects of the outer scene provoke a tragic memory: the intimations of impermanence noted above and the scene's seclusion ("un site écarté"; "ce sentier perdu;" "ce désert immense"). As in Wordsworth's *Tintern Abbey* the secluded scene impresses "thoughts of more deep seclusion." And as in both *Tintern Abbey* and *Souvenir* demonstrative adjectives are frequent and serve as shifters as well as pointers, that is, they shift the emphasis from objective contemplation of nature to subjective experience (see *supra*, pp. 108 f.f.). Intermingled with the natural setting

170

are the eyes of his estranged mistress which follow him everywhere, even to this remote setting.

> Ote-moi, mémoire importune,
> Ote-moi ces yeux que je vois toujours!
>   (23-24)

There are no fewer than six of these apostrophes in the poem. Apostrophe is a typical feature of the greater Romantic lyric; it is, as Jonathan Culler has noted, a sign of the genre and of the genre's sublime register.

The memory brings on a feeling of tragic loss.

> Pourquoi, dans leur beauté suprême,
> Pourquoi les ai-je vus briller?
>   (25-26)

Then the poet neglects entirely the natural scene before him, thinking only now of his former mistress and addressing her directly.

> Tu ne veux plus que je les aime,
> Toi qui me défends d'oublier!
>   (27-28)

(3) In the next movement the speaker tries to face up to his tragic loss. He focuses his attention on, and will try immediately to emulate, the "eternal calm" of the mountains.

> Comme après la douleur, comme après la tempête
> L'homme supplie encore et regarde le ciel,
> Le voyageur, lèvant la tete,
> Vit les Alpes debout dans leur calme éternel.
>   (29-32)

He notices now that the sun is "paisible et fort à l'aise." He tells himself not to fear the abyss below nor the avalanche above, in both the literal and figurative sense of course. His self-admonition is working: the songs and the tears of Italy are "already the past," that is, the tragic memory, while not erased, is already beginning to lose its sting.

(4) A frequently recurring structural element in the greater Romantic lyric is the return, after a painful memory and meditation, to the natural scene but with an altered mood or deepened understanding. In *Souvenir des Alpes* it is the Alpine forest that offers the final instructive lesson and brings on the altered mood. Where Byron saw the giant fir trees as sepulchral ("cet air de cimetière"), reminding him only of dead friends, Musset sees their grandiose beauty and their calm repose.

> Peut-être en savent-ils autant et plus que nous,
> Ces vieux êtres muets attachés à la terre,
> Qui, sur le sein fécond de la commune mère,
> Dorment dans un repos si superbe et si doux. (69-72)

The passage is saturated with the pathetic fallacy, allowing Nature to become a wise teacher and the observer a willing pupil. The link between the tall trees, often hit by lightening, and the poet is the epithet *foudroyés*, which echoes the *brisé* applied to the latter in the first line. The poet clearly sees the lesson to be learned from the noble forest: he must resolve his emotional problem, he must seek equanimity or at least emotional equilibrium and become, like the pines, "attached" to Mother Earth.

The mood, then, has definitely altered; the poet has achieved a deeper understanding of his grief, and it is Nature that has helped him put his grief behind him. An earlier line had already foreshadowed the change.

> L'ardent soleil séchait les larmes de ses yeux.
> (20)

The epithet *ardent* not only smuggles in still another instance of the pathetic fallacy, but also establishes, surreptitiously, still another link between subject and object.

The altered mood is also reflected in the prosody. Until the final stanza the poem had nervously alternated between lines of 12, 10, 8 and 6 syllables. The last stanza, so different thematically from the initial one that presented a "broken" traveler with broken rhythms (e.g., 2+3+5), now uses the stately alexandrine and the perfectly balanced median caesura (6+6), thus creating a rhythm more appropriate to the poet's new-found sense of equilibrium.

NOTES

chapter one

1. Valentine Brunet (*Le Lyrisme d'Alfred de Musset*) finds evidence that Musset's sorceress, Belisa (in *Don Paez*), may have been influenced by *La Celestina* of Fernando de Rojas. See Brunet for a more detailed account of Musset's Spanish sources.
2. Alfred de Musset, *Poésies complètes*, ed. Maurice Allem (Paris: Gallimard, 1957), p. 36. All subsequent quotations from Musset's poetry are taken from this edition. References to line numbers are given only for the detailed stylistic analyses in Part Two. Purely documentary information following quotations from secondary sources are placed in the text rather than in notes. The information includes only the name of the author, a short or shortened title and page number. For full bibliographical information, including name of publisher, date and place of publication, consult the Bibliography.
3. For a discussion of the romantic hero as *puer senex*, see my recent book, *The Romantic Hero and his Heirs in French Literature* (Bern: Peter Lang, 1984), pp. 13-15.
4. See Margaret Rees' introduction to her edition of *Les Contes d'Espagne et d'Italie* (London: Athlone Press, 1973), p. 27.

chapter two

1. Quoted by Maurice Allem in the *Poésies complètes*, p. 730.
2. For a discussion of the romantic hero as orphan see my study of *The Romantic Hero and his Heirs*, pp. 15-16.

chapter four

1. See Hermine B. Riffaterre, *Orphisme dans la poésie romantique* (Paris: Nizet, 1970), pp. 125-26, for a discussion of such imagery in connection with Musset.
2. For a recent discussion of the organic philosophy of the romantics, see Hans Eichner, "The Rise of Modern Science and the Genesis of Romanticism," *PMLA*, 97 (January, 1982), 8-30.

chapter five

1. Alfred de Musset, *Poésies complètes*, p. 83. References in arabic numerals are to line numbers.

2. I shall use the semiotic approach of Michael Riffaterre as developed in his *Semiotics of Poetry* (Bloomington: Indiana University Press, 1978) and *La Production du texte* (Paris: Seuil, 1979).

3. See Nicolas Ruwet, "Parallelism and Deviation in Poetry," in *French Literary Theory Today*, ed. Tzvetan Todorov (Cambridge: Cambridge University Press, 1982), pp. 92-124.

4. See *La Production du texte*, pp. 76 and 161.

chapter six

1. Henri Peyre, *Literature and Sincerity* (New Haven: Yale University Press, 1963), p. 141.

2. Sylvan Barnet et al, *A Dictionary of Literary Terms* (Boston: Little Brown, 1960), pp. 51-52.

3. Raymond Immerwahr, "The Subjectivity or Objectivity of Friedrich Schlegel's Poetic Irony," *Germanic Review*, 26 (1951), 177.

4. See Morton Gurewitch, "European Romantic Irony," Diss. Columbia, 1957, p. 6.

5. John P. Houston (*The Demonic Imagination*) and Pierre Moreau ("L'Ironie de Musset") have characterized Musset as a "romantic ironist", but no one has yet seen fit to analyze *Namouna* in terms of romantic irony.

6. References in roman numerals are to cantos, those in arabic numerals are to stanzas.

7. Lord Byron, fragment on the back of the poet's manuscript for the first canto of *Don Juan*.

8. As Hubert Juin has said, in so far as the hero, as hero, is deconstructed, the poem, as a linear narrative contiuum, is likewise deconstructed. See Hubert Juin, "Le Poème d'Alfred de Musset," *Europe*, 55, no. 583-84 (nov.-déc. 1977), 150.

9. See Maurice Allem, note 37 in Musset's *Poesies complètes*, pp. 705-06.

10. See Pierre Fortassier, "L'Expression indirecte du réel et sa théorie chez Valéry, La Fontaine, Musset," *L'Information Littéraire*, 20, 15-16.

chapter seven

1. For Coleridge, Wordsworth, Keats and Shelley, see M. W. Abrams, "Structure and Style in the Greater Romantic Lyric," in *From Sensibility to Romanticism: Essays Presented to Frederick A. Pottle*,

eds. Frederick W. Hilles and Harold Bloom (New York: Oxford University Press, 1965), p. 527. Reprinted in *Romanticism and Consciousness*, ed. Harold Bloom (New York: Norton, 1971), pp. 453-57.

2. For *Tristesse d'Olympio*, see Patricia A. Ward, "*Tristesse d'Olympio* and the Romantic Nature Experience," *Nineteenth-Century French Studies*, 7 (1978-79), 4-6. For *Le Lac*, see Lloyd Bishop, "*Le Lac* and the Greater *Romantic Lyric*," to appear in the *Kentucky Romance Quarterly*.

3. For Yeats, see George Bornstein, "Yeats and the Greater Romantic Lyric," in *Romantic and Modern: Revaluations of Literary Tradition* (Pittsburgh: University of Pittsburgh Press, 1977), 91-110. For the others, see Abrams, "Greater Romantic Lyric," 529.

4. Alfred de Musset, *Poésies complètes*, p. 404.

chapter eight

1. See Lila Maurice-Amour, "Musset, la musique et les musiciens," *Revue des Sciences Humaines*, 89 (1958), 31-58.

2. Lloyd Bishop, "Phonological Correlates of Euphony," *The French Review* 49 (October 1975), especially pp. 12-15, 17, 21-22. This essay was expanded in my book, *In Search of Style* (Charlottesville: University Press of Virginia, 1982), chapter four.

3. Ibid., pp. 386-87. See also, Grammont's *Petit traité de versification française* (Paris: Armand Colin, 1967), p. 140.

4. Mario Pei, *The Story of Language* (New York: New American Library, 1966), pp. 113-14.

5. Although he warns against the abuse of rhyme in his famous manifesto, "Art poétique," Verlaine nonetheless believed that French poetry could not dispense with it since the relatively unaccented French language needs the extra stress.

6. See M. Gauthier, "Cinq principes fondamentaux d'euphonie des vers français," *Information Littéraire*, 25, no. 5 (nov.-déc., 1973), 217-18.

7. For this and the following two charts, see Morier, op. cit, pp. 246-48.

chapter nine

1. For a lengthy discussion of initial critical reaction to the *Contes*, see Pierre Gastinel, *Le Romantisme d'Alfred de Musset* (Paris:

Hachette, 1933), pp. 129-48. Unless otherwise indicated all excerpts from critical reviews of 1830 are taken from this passage.

2. Quoted by Simon Jeune, *Musset et sa fortune littéraire* (Bordeaux: Ducros, 1970), p. 11. This is a book-length discussion of critical reaction to Musset's entire opus from 1830 to 1970. References to texts quoted by Jeune will be abbreviated as *FL*. Patricia Siegel's recent bibliographical guide (*Musset: A Reference Guide*, 1982), now the most complete and up to date, extends to 1982. References to Siegel's bibliography will be abbreviated as *MRG*.

3. See for instance René Doumic, "Le classicisme de Musset," *Revue des deux mondes*, 15 juin 1907, 923-24. Other critics who have written on Musset's classicism are Pierre Moreau, Emile Henriot, Jean Thomas, Anatole Claveau, Paul Fort, René Groos, Ann S. Courtney.

BIBLIOGRAPHY

The bibliography lists all works cited and a few others consulted, the latter mainly in the areas of literary theory and recent developments in literary criticism. Some forty works on Musset, articles mainly, that were not found helpful are not listed, but they might be of interest to future researchers working on Musset's poetry; they can be found in Patricia Siegel's monumental bibliography on Musset (*Alfred de Musset: A Reference Guide*, 1982). Siegel's work supersedes all other bibliographies on Musset.

Abrams, Myer W. "Structure and Style in the Greater Romantic Lyric." in *From Sensibility to Romanticism: Essays Presented to Frederick A. Pottle*, eds. Frederick W. Hillis and Harold Bloom. New York: Oxford University Press, 1965, pp. 527-560.

Adam, Antoine. "Son romantisme est le nôtre." *Nouvelles Littéraires*, 9 May, 1957, 4.

Allem, Maurice. *Musset*. Paris: Nouvelle Revue Critique, 1940.

Aragon (Louis). "Alfred de Musset 1857-1957: sous les cyprès anciens que de saules nouveaux!" *Les Lettres Françaises*, no. 667 (18 April 1957), 1, 12.

Aquitaine, Jean d.' *Alfred de Musset: l'oeuvre, le poète*. Paris: Gaillard, 1907.

Bailey, R.W. et al. *The Sign: Semiotics Around the World*. Ann Arbor: Michigan Slavic Publications, 1978.

Barat, Emmanuel. *Le style poétique et la révolution romantique*. Paris: Hachette, 1904.

Barine, Arvède. *Alfred de Musset*. Paris: Hachette, 1893.

Barnet, Sylvan et al. *A Dictionary of Literary Terms*. Boston: Little Brown, 1960.

Berteau, Rolande. "Procédés de revivification des comparaisons traditionnelles de renforcement dans les Premières Poésies d'Alfred de Musset." In *Linguistique romane et linguistique française: Hommages à Jacques Pohl*. Ed. Marc Dominicy and Marc Wilmet. Brussels: Editions de L'Université de Bruxelles, 1980, 39-46.

Bishop, Lloyd. "Phonological Correlates of Euphony." *The French Review*, 49 (October, 1975), 11-21.

_____ "Romantic Irony in Musset's *Souvenir*" *Nineteenth-Century French Studies*, 7 (Spring-Summer 1979), 181-91.

_____ *In Search of Style: Essays in French Literary Stylistics*. Charlottesville: University Press of Virginia, 1982.

———————— *The Romantic Hero and his Heirs in French Literature.*
Bern: Peter Lang, 1984.

———————— "Musset's *Souvenir* and the Greater Romantic Lyric."
Nineteenth-Century French Studies, 12 (Spring-Summer, 1984), 119-
130.

Bornstein, George. "Yeats and the Greater Romantic Lyric." In *Romantic
and Modern: Revaluations of Literary Tradition.* Pittsburgh: University
of Pittsburgh Press, 1977, pp. 91-110.

Bourget, Paul. *Sociologie et littérature.* Paris: Plon, 1906.

Brereton, Geoffrey. "Alfred de Musset." In his *An Introduction to the
French Poets.* London: Methuen, 1956, pp. 137-47.

Brunet, Valentine. *Le lyrisme d'Alfred de Musset dans ses poésies.*
Toulouse: Imprimerie Régionale, 1932.

Brunetière, Ferdinand. *L'Evolution de la poésie lyrique au XIXe Siècle.*
Paris: Hachette, 1895.

Cassou, Jean. *Les Nuits de Musset.* Paris: Emile-Paul, 1930.

Charpentier, John. *Alfred de Musset.* Paris: Tallandier, 1928.

Citron, Pierre. *La poésie de Paris dans la littérature française de Rousseau
à Baudelaire.* Paris: Editions de Minuit, 1961. Vol. I.

Claveau, André. *Alfred de Musset.* Paris: Lecène et Oudin, 1894.

Culler, Jonathan. *Structuralist Poetics.* London: Routledge and Kegan
Paul, 1975.

———————— *The Pursuit of Signs: Semiotics, Literature,
Deconstruction.* Ithaca: Cornell University Press, 1981.

———————— *On Deconstruction: Theory and Criticism after
Structuralism.* Ithaca: Cornell University Press, 1982.

Daemmrich, I. G. "Musset's View of the Poet." *Revue des langues vivantes,*
19 (1973), 5-10.

De Man, Paul. *Allegories of Reading: Figural Language in Rousseau,
Nietzsche, Rilke, and Proust.* New York: Yale University Press, 1979.

Denommé, Robert T. *Nineteenth-Century French Romantic Poets.*
Carbondale: Southern Illinois University Press, 1969.

Dolder, Charlotte. *Le thème de l'être et du paraître dans l'itinéraire
spirituel de Musset.* Zurich: Juris-Verlag, 1968.

Donnay, Maurice. *Alfred de Musset.* Paris: Hachette, 1914.

Doumic, René. "Le classicisme de Musset." *Revue des Deux Mondes,*
15 June 1907, 923-24.

Dussane, Mme Beatrix et al. "Lit-on encore et aime-t-on, dans Musset,
les poèmes?" *Le Figaro littéraire,* 4 May 1957, 1, 5.

Eichner, Hans. "The Rise of Modern Science and the Genesis of Romanticism." *PMLA*, 97 (January 1982), 8-22.

Forrest-Thomson, Veronica. "Levels of Poetic Convention." *Journal of European Studies*, 2 (1972), 35-51.

Fortassier, Pierre. "L'expression indirecte du réel et sa théorie chez Valéry, La Fontaine, Musset." *L'Information Littéraire*, 20, 7-17.

Fournet, Charles. *Poètes romantiques: études littéraires*. Geneva: Georg, 1962.

Fowlie, Wallace. *The French Critic 1549-1967*. Carbondale: Southern Illinois University Press, 1968.

Frohock, W.M. "Euphony." In his *French Literature: An Approach through Close Reading*. Cambridge, Mass: Schoenhof's, 1964, pp. 58-61.

Frye, Northrop, ed. *Sound and Poetry*. New York: Columbia University Press, 1956.

Galdi, Ladislas. "Un aspect peu connu du style poétique de Musset." *Cahiers de l'Association Internationale des Etudes Françaises*, 16 (1964), 21-30.

Ganne, Gilbert. *Alfred de Musset: Sa jeunesse et la nôtre*. Paris: Librairie Perrin, 1970.

Gastinel, Françoise. "Critique et Poète: Sainte-Beuve et Alfred de Musset." In *Mélanges d'histoire littéraire et de bibliographie offerts à Jean Bonnerot*. Paris: Nizet, 1954, pp. 231-35.

Gastinel, Pierre. *Le Romantisme d'Alfred de Musset*. Paris: Hachette, 1933.

Gauthier-Ferrières. *Alfred de Musset: Vie et oeuvre*. Paris: Larousse, 1909.

Gauthier, M. "Cinq principes fondamentaux d'euphonie des vers français." *L'Information Littéraire*, 25, no. 5 (nov.-déc. 1973), 212-218.

Giraud, Victor. "Pour le centenaire des *Nuits*." *Revue des Deux Mondes*, 33 (1936), 452-465.

Gobineau, Comte de. *Etudes critiques*. Paris: Simon Kra, n.d.

Grammont, Maurice. *Essai de psychologie linguistique: Style et poésie*. Paris: Delagrave, 1950.

_____ *Le Vers français: ses moyens d'expression, son harmonie*. Paris: Delagrave, 1967.

_____ *Petit traité de versification française*. Paris: Armand Colin, 1967.

Greet, Anne H. "Humor in the Poetry of Alfred de Musset." *Studies in Romanticism*, 6, no. 3 (Spring 1967), 75-92.

Guillemain, Henri. "Notes sur Musset." *Temps Modernes*, 18, 447-83.

Gurewitch, Morton. "European Romantic Irony." Diss. Columbia, 1957.

Han, Françoise. "Quelques notes sur *Namouna* et sur la rhétorique." *Europe*, 55, no. 583-84 (nov.-déc. 1977), 170-74.

Haven, Richard. "Some Perspectives in Three Poems by Gray, Wordsworth, and Duncan." In *Romantic and Modern: Revaluations of Literary Tradition.* Pittsburg: University of Pittsburg Press, 1977, pp. 69-88.

Henriot, Emile. *Alfred de Musset.* Paris: Hachette, 1928.

Hershensohn, Michael. "Imagery in the works of Alfred de Musset." Diss. Pennsylvania, 1971.

Hewitt, James R. "The Tropes of Self in the Poetry of Alfred de Musset." Diss. New York University, 1973.

Houston, John P. *The Demonic Imagination: Style and Theme in French Romantic Poetry.* Baton Rouge: Louisiana State University Press, 1969.

Immerwahr, Raymond. "The Subjectivity or Objectivity of Friedrich Schlegel's Poetic Irony." *Germanic Review*, 26 (1951), 173-91.

James Henry. *French Poets and Novelists.* London: MacMillan, 1878.

Janzé, Vicomtesse de. *Etudes et récits sur Alfred de Musset.* Paris: Plon, 1891.

Jeune, Simon. *Musset et sa fortune littéraire.* Bordeaux: Dueros, 1970.

———————— "Aspects de la narration dans les premières poésies d'Alfred de Musset." *Revue d'Histoire Littéraire de la France*, 76, 179-91.

Juin, Hubert. "Le poème d'Alfred de Musset." *Europe*, 55, no. 583-84 (nov-déc. 1977), 147-54.

King, Russell S. "Indecision in Musset's *Contes d'Espagne et d'Italie*" *Nottingham French Studies*, 8, 57-68.

———————— "Musset: the Poet of Dionysus. *Studies in Romanticism*, 13 (1974), 323-32.

———————— "Musset et le dialogue nietzschéen d'Appolon et de Dionysos." *Europe*, 55, no. 583-84 (nov.-déc. 1977), 162-69.

Lainey, Yves. *Musset ou la difficulté d'aimer.* Paris: Société d'Edition d'Enseignement Supérieur, 1978.

Lamartine, Alphonse. *Cours familier de littérature.* 18e entretien. Paris: "chez l'auteur," 1857.

Lefèbvre, Henri. *Musset.* Paris: L'Arche, 1956.

Le Hir, Yves. "L'Expression du sentiment amoureux dans l'oeuvre poétique d'Alfred de Musset." *Le Français Moderne*, 23 (1955), 176-190 and 275-279; 24 (1956), 15-34.

Le Sage, Laurent. *The French New Criticism*. University Park: The Pennsylvania State University Press, 1967.

Levin, Samuel R. "The Conventions of Poetry." *In Literary Style: A Symposium*. Ed. Seymour Chatman. London: Oxford University Press, 1971.

Marouzeau, J. *Précis de stylistique française*. Paris: Masson, 1950.

Masson, Bernard. "Relire les *Nuits* de Musset sous la lumière de Jung." *Revue d'Histoire Littéraire de la France*, 76, 192-210.

Maurice-Amour, Lila. "Musset et la musique." *Les Nouvelles Littéraires* 9 May, 1957, 10.

——————— "Musset, la musique et les musiciens." *Revue des Sciences Humaines*, no. 89 (1958), 31-54.

——————— "Esquisse d'une bibliographie musicale de l'oeuvre d'Alfred de Musset." *Revue des Sciences Humaines*, no. 89 (1958), 55-58.

Maurois, André. "Musset cent ans après: discuté mais vivant." *Les Nouvelles Littéraires*, 9 May 1957, 1, 5.

Merlant, Joachim, ed. *Musset: Morceaux choisis*. Paris: Didier, 1924.

Molho, Raphaël. "L'automne et le printemps: Sainte-Beuve, juge de Musset." *Revue des Sciences Humaines*, numéro spécial, no. 108 (Oct-Dec. 1962), 637-50.

Montégut, Emile. *Nos Morts contemporains*. Paris: Hachette, 1893.

Moreau, Pierre. *Le classicisme des romantiques*. Paris: Plon, 1932.

——————— "L'Ironie de Musset." *Revue des Sciences Humaines*, numéro spécial, no. 108 (Oct.-Dec. 1962), 501-514.

——————— *Ames et thèmes romantiques*. Paris: Corti, 1965.

Morier, Henri. *Dictionnaire de poétique et de rhétorique*. Paris: Presses Universitaires de France, 1975.

Musset, Alfred de. *Correspondance d'Alfred de Musset*. Ed. Léon Seché. Paris: Mercure de France, 1907.

——————— *Lettres d'Amour à Aimée d'Alton*. Paris: Mercure de France, 1910.

——————— *Poésies complètes*. Ed. Maurice Allem. Paris: Gallimard, 1957.

——————— *Oeuvres complètes en prose*. Ed. Maurice Allem. Paris: Gallimard, 1960.

——————— *Oeuvres complètes*. Ed. Philippe Van Tieghem. Paris: Seuil, 1963.

Musset, Paul de. *Biographie d'Alfred de Musset*. In *Musset: Oeuvres complètes*. Ed. Philippe Van Tieheem. Paris: Seuil, 1963.

Nist, John. "The Ontology of Style." *Linguistics*, 42 (1968), 44-57.

Norris, Christopher. *Deconstruction: Theory and Practice*. London: Meuthuen, 1982.

Odoul, Pierre. *Le drame intime d'Alfred de Musset*. Paris: Pensée Universelle, 1974.

Oxenhandler, Neal. *French Literary Criticism: The Basis of Judgment*. Englewood Cliffs: Prentice-Hall, 1966.

Pei, Mario. *The Story of Language*. New York: New American Library, 1966.

Peyre, Henri. *Literature and Sincerity*. New York: Yale University Press, 1963.

Pichois, Claude. *Philarète Chasle et la vie littéraire au temps du romantisme*. Paris: José Corti, 1965. Vol. I.

Poli, Annaros. "La critique italienne de Musset." *Europe*, 55, no. 583-84, 193-202.

Poulet, Georges. *Les Métamorphoses du cercle*. Paris: Plon, 1961.

—————————— *La distance intérieure*. Paris: Plon, 1964.

Pommier, Jean. *Alfred de Musset*. Oxford: Clarendon Press, 1957.

Porter, Laurence. *The Renaissance of the Lyric in French Romanticism: Elegy,"Poème", and Ode*. French Forum, Lexington Kentucky, 1978.

Rees, Margaret. *Alfred de Musset*. New York: Twayne, 1971.

—————————— , ed. "Introduction" to her edition of *Contes d'Espagne et d'Italie*. London: Athline Press, 1973, pp. 1-34.

Reboul, Pierre. "Sur cinq à six marches de marbre rose." *Revue des Sciences Humaines*, numéro spécial, no. 108 (Oct.-Dec. 1962), 627-36.

—————————— "Le poète contre la poésie." *Europe*, 55, no. 583-84 (Nov-Dec. 1977), 155-62.

Richard, Jean-Pierre. *Etudes sur le romantisme*. Paris: Seuil, 1970.

Riffaterre, Hermine B. *Orphisme dans la poésie romantique*. Paris: Nizet, 1970.

Riffaterre, Michael. *Semiotics of Poetry*. Bloomington: Indiana University Press, 1978.

—————————— *La Production du texte*. Paris: Seuil, 1979.

Rudrauf, Lucien. "Structure consonantique de la musique verbale." *Revue d'Esthétique*, 3 (1950), 1-28.

Ruwet, Nicolas. "Parallelism and Deviation in Poetry." In *French Literary Theory Today*. Ed. Tzvetan Todorov. Cambridge: Cambridge University Press, 1982, pp. 92-124.

Sainte-Beuve, Charles Augustin. *Portraits contemporains.* Paris: Calmann-Lévy, 1877. Vol. II.

―――――――― *Causeries du lundi.* Paris: Garnier Frères, 1883. Vol. XIII.

Séché, Léon. *Alfred de Musset.* 2 vols. Paris: Mercure de France, 1907.

Siegel, Patricia J. "Structure et thématique dans la poésie d'Alfred de Musset." Diss. Yale, 1970.

―――――――― "Deux frères spirituels d'Alfred de Musset." *Romance Notes,* 16 (1974), 46-54.

―――――――― "Musset, protagoniste de l'avenir." *Nineteenth-Century French Studies,* 4, no. 3, 220-32.

―――――――― "Musset's *Souvenir:* Hugo or Dante?" *Les bonnes feuilles,* 8, no. 1, 3-15.

―――――――― *Alfred de Musset: A Reference Guide.* Boston: G.K. Hall, 1982.

Simon, John K., ed. *Modern French Criticism: from Proust and Valéry to Structuralism.* Chicago: University of Chicago Press, 1972.

Soupault, Philippe. *Alfred de Musset.* Paris: Seghers, 1957.

Spire, André. *Plaisir poétique, plaisir musculaire.* New York: S.F. Vanni, 1949.

Stankiewicz, Edward. "Centripetal and Centrifugal Structures in Poetry." *Semiotica,* 38, no. 3-4 (1982) 217-42.

Stapfer, Paul. *Alfred de Musset.* Guernesey, 1869.

Starobinski, Jean. *L'oeil vivant.* Paris: Gallimard, 1961. Vol. II.

Sutcliffe, M. "A Study of Musset's Vocabulary and Imagery." Diss. Leeds, 1961.

Swinburne, A.C. "Tennyson and Musset." In his *Miscellanies.* London: Chatto and Windus, 1886, 219-59.

Todorov, Tzvetan, ed. *French Literary Theory Today.* Cambridge: Cambridge University Press, 1982.

Toesca, Maurice. *Alfred de Musset ou l'amour de la mort.* Paris: Hachette, 1970.

Tompkins, Jane, ed. *Reader-Response Criticism: from Formalism to Post-Structuralism.* Baltimore: The Johns Hopkins University Press, 1980.

Van Tieghem, Philippe. *Musset.* Paris: Hatier, 1969.

Ward, Patricia A. "*Tristesse d'Olympio* and the Romantic Nature Experience." *Nineteenth-Century French Studies,* 7 (1978-79), 4-6.

Warren, Robert Penn. "Pure and Impure Poetry." *The Kenyon Review* (Spring, 1943), 228-254.

Zola, Emile. "Souvenirs." in *Nouveaux Contes à Ninon*. Paris: Charpentier, 1874, pp. 166-68.

INDEX

Lloyd Bishop

THE ROMANTIC HERO AND HIS HEIRS IN FRENCH LITERATURE

American University Studies: Series II, Romance Languages and Literature, Vol. 10

ISBN 0-8204-0096-3   297 pp.   hardback   US $ 32,50

Recommended price - alterations reserved

Our contemporary view of the romantic hero is blurred by infrequently examined assumptions. The purpose of Professor Bishop's book on *The Romantic Hero and his Heirs* is two-fold: to draw a precise and updated portrait of the original romantic hero in French literature and then to trace his legitimate heirs from the romantic period to the middle of the twentieth century – and beyond. By bringing together his own findings and those of other scholars he establishes the important fact of literary history that *the romantic hero is the central hero of modern French literature.* The book offers not only a detailed description and genealogy of a significant literary hero, it also provides a description of the modern sensibility. This is an ambitious and convincing work of vast and precise erudition.

Contents: A precise and updated portrait of the romantic hero in French Literature and of his legitimate heirs from the romantic period to the middle of the twentieth century – and beyond.

PETER LANG PUBLISHING, INC.
62 West 45th Street
USA - New York, NY 10036